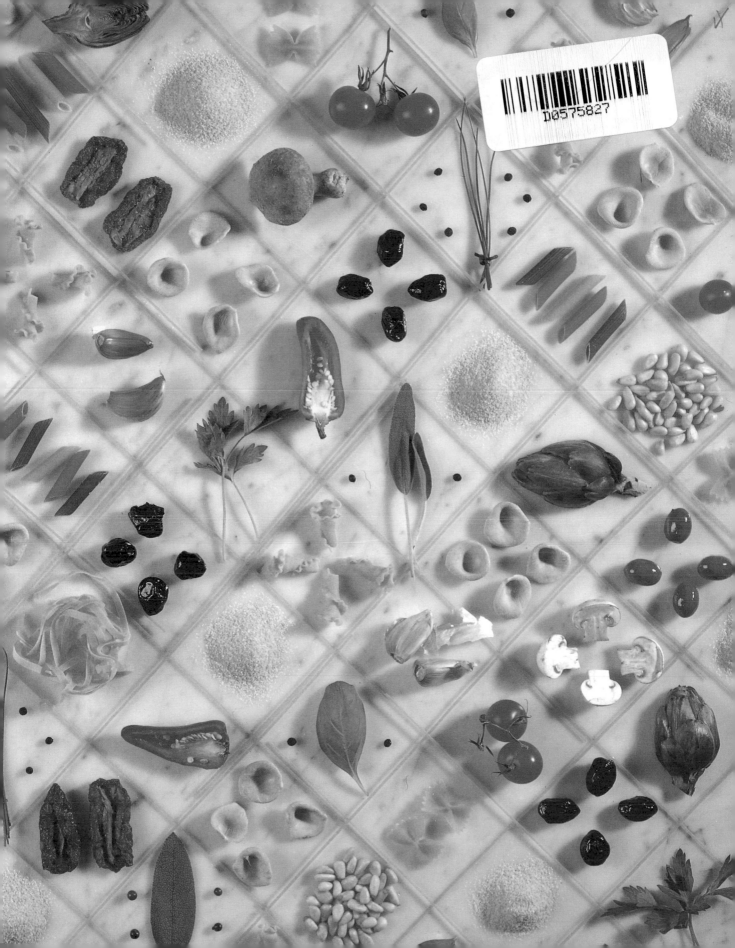

D0575827

Pizza, Pasta and Polenta

URSULA FERRIGNO
Pizza, Pasta
and Polenta

MEREHURST

DEDICATION

I dedicate this book to my three sisters, Gina, Nicola and Andrea, who, like Pizza, Pasta and Polenta, play a major part in my life.

ACKNOWLEDGEMENTS

I would like to thank – MY GRANDMOTHER for her inspiration and teaching from a very young age. GIULIANO FILIPPI and ANDREAS LAGLER for their help. MICHELE BARLOW for testing the recipes and all her support. LINDA SHANKS and FIONA LINDSAY for being not only excellent agents but also for their intuition. GILL MACLENNAN for thinking of such a brilliant title and suggesting that I write this book. SUSANNA TEE for again tirelessly editing, her great spirit and total dedication and professionalism. JENNY AND DAVE ROBERTS from Premium Services for all their excellent typing and computer skills. GALBANI CHEESES for their delicious cheese used in my recipes. BODUM COOKWARE for generously supplying me with equipment for my cookery demonstrations.

Published in 1995 by Merehurst Ltd
Ferry House, 51-57 Lacy Road, Putney, London SW15 1PR

Copyright 1995 © Ursula Ferrigno
Reprinted 1996

ISBN 1-85391-468-1

All rights reserved. No part of this publication may be reproduced, stored in a retrieval system, or transmitted in any form or by any means, electronic, mechanical, photocopying or otherwise, without the prior written permission of the copyright owner.

A catalogue record for this book is available from the British Library.

Editor: Susanna Tee
Art direction and design: Hammond Hammond
Photographer: Alan Marsh
Home economist: Louise Pickford
Stylist: Fiona Tillett
Typesetter: Mike Weintroub

Colour separation by Toppan
Printed in Singapore by Toppan

NOTES

A standard spoon measurement is used in all recipes:

1 teaspoon = one 5 ml spoon
1 tablespoon = one 15 ml spoon
All spoon measures are level.

All eggs are size 3 unless otherwise specified.

For all recipes, quantities are given in metric and imperial. Follow one set of measures but not a mixture as they are not interchangeable.

Pizza

11

Pasta

43

Polenta

85

*I**taly captures your heart.* The food, countryside and atmosphere offer something special and you will want to return again and again. The complete contrast in the weather of northern, central and southern Italy makes the food full of character and colour.

Pasta binds Italy from north to south and is fundamental to Italian life and gastronomy. Northern food has touches of German, French and Austrian influences and due to the colder climate, the food is richer and more dairy orientated. Polenta comes from this part of Italy. In Central Italy, they enjoy porcini and the black truffles of Norcia. From Rome and southern Italy where the weather is warmer, lighter, colourful food, such as Pizza, is popular.

I know that the recipes in this book are pure. They are the food that the Italians eat and enjoy on a daily basis. I would like these recipes to be part of your everyday life so that you can enjoy their gastronomic delights. It is simple food, lovingly cooked and presented. It comes from the heart.

Ursula Ferrigno

Pizza

PIZZAS are so easy to make and immensely satisfying. There is no special secret but there are some very simple rules which I am keen to pass on to you.

The flour used is important. It should be made from hard durum wheat which, when milled, produces a strong flour, rich in gluten. This is finely milled to produce 'O' grade flour which gives the best results for pizzas. You can buy 'O' grade flour from Italian food shops, good delicatessens and some large supermarkets. If you can't get hold of it, use ordinary strong bread flour. Plain flour, used for pastries and sauces, doesn't work well. Kneading too is important and you should use your hands to soften and stretch the dough.

Pizzas do not have to be large and round. Some are rectangular, some are oval and some are small individual rounds called pizzette. Some even have a deep crust and sides like a pie which, after all, is what pizza means – pie.

Choose your topping carefully. A good pizza is a happy marriage of flavours – don't be tempted to pile too many things on at once.

Keep it simple.

Pizza dough

15 g (½ oz) fresh yeast or 1½ teaspoons dried
yeast and a pinch of sugar

about 50 ml (2 fl oz) hand-hot water

250 g (8 oz) strong white unbleached flour,
preferably 'O' grade

½ teaspoon sea salt

50 ml (2 fl oz) olive oil

SERVES 4 – 6

TIP Fresh yeast can be bought in most
health food shops and in supermarkets that
have their own instore bakery.

1. Blend the fresh yeast with a little of the
hand-hot water. (If using dried yeast,
sprinkle it into a little of the water with the
sugar and leave in a warm place for 15
minutes until frothy).

2. Sift the flour and salt well together.
Make a reservoir in the centre and add the
oil, yeast liquid and some of the water. Mix
together with a wooden spoon, gradually
adding the remaining water, to form a soft
dough.

3. Turn the dough out on to a lightly
floured surface and knead vigorously for 10
minutes until the dough is soft and satiny
(don't be afraid of adding more flour).

4. Lightly oil a large bowl, then roll the
dough around it to cover the surface of the
dough with oil. Cover the bowl with a clean
tea-towel and leave in a warm place for 1½
hours, until doubled in size.

Rolling and baking pizza dough

Risen pizza dough, doubled in size, now ready for rolling and baking.

1. Knock down the dough with your knuckles then remove from bowl. Knead on a very lightly floured surface for 2 - 3 minutes to knock out the air bubbles.

2. On a very lightly floured surface, preferably marble, roll out the dough very, very thinly – as thin as a paper napkin folded in four. (This quantity of dough will produce a 25 - 30 cm (10 - 12 in) round pizza).

3. Now add your favourite topping.

4. Place the dough on to a hot baking sheet, terracotta pizza stone, some clean oiled bricks or unglazed quarry tiles in the bottom of your oven. (I recommend these as they will enable you to achieve a perfect crisp crust just like an Italian pizza).

5. Bake in a pre-heated oven at 200C (400F/Gas 6) for 20 - 25 minutes until golden and crisp.

Char-grilled vegetable pizza

This pizza is a lovely combination of flavours and colours. While the dough is rising and resting you can grill the courgettes and aubergines and skin and chop the tomatoes. The rocket adds a lovely peppery flavour and softens gently with the heat of the topping.

1 quantity of Pizza Dough (see page 12)

1 medium courgette

1 medium aubergine

4 tablespoons olive oil

8 tomatoes

sea salt and freshly ground black pepper

100 g (4 oz) mozzarella cheese

handful of fresh basil leaves, torn

handful of rocket

SERVES 4 – 6

1. Prepare the pizza dough as described on page 12.

2. Cut the courgette lengthways, into 7.5 cm (3 in) slices. Cut the aubergine lengthways into 10 cm (4 in) slices. Brush the courgette and aubergine lengths with some of the oil and grill using medium heat for 4 - 5 minutes on each side.

3. Put the tomatoes in a bowl, cover with boiling water for about 40 seconds then plunge into cold water. Using a sharp knife, peel off the skins. Chop the flesh and season with salt and pepper. Slice the mozzarella cheese.

4. Preheat the oven to 200C (400F/Gas 6). On a very lightly floured surface, roll out the pizza dough very thinly into a round. Place on an oiled baking sheet.

5. Brush the pizza base with the remaining oil. Sprinkle over the basil. Add the chopped tomatoes then arrange the aubergine, courgette and cheese slices on top.

6. Bake in the oven for 20 - 25 minutes until golden and bubbling. Arrange rocket on top of pizza and serve.

TIP Another herb that I sometimes use, instead of the basil, is fresh oregano.

Aubergine and ricotta pizza

Anyone familiar with my first book, 'The 90s Vegetarian', will know of my love of aubergines. Here is another one of my favourite aubergine recipes. I think it is important to salt and rinse the aubergines. Firstly because aubergines are part of the Deadly Nightshade family and the beads of liquid you draw out are bitter. Secondly, the aubergines absorb less oil afterwards.

1 quantity of Pizza Dough (see page 12)

½ medium aubergine

sea salt and freshly ground black pepper

4 ripe tomatoes

1 small red onion

2 tablespoons olive oil

25 g (1 oz) freshly grated Parmesan cheese

250 g (8 oz) ricotta

handful of fresh basil leaves

SERVES 4 – 6

1. Prepare the pizza dough as described on page 12.

2. Slice the aubergine lengthways. Put the slices in a colander, sprinkle with salt, cover and weigh down. Leave for 30 minutes.

3. Meanwhile, put the tomatoes in a bowl, cover with boiling water for about 40 seconds then plunge into cold water. Skin then slice the tomatoes.

4. Slice the onion into rings. Heat half the oil in a saucepan, add the rings and fry until softened. Add the tomatoes, salt and pepper and set aside.

5. Rinse the aubergine slices and pat dry. Brush the slices with the remaining oil and grill using medium heat for 10 minutes, turning once until lightly cooked.

6. Preheat the oven to 200C (400F/Gas 6). On a very lightly floured surface, roll out the pizza dough very thinly into a round. Place on an oiled baking sheet.

7. Brush the pizza with the remaining oil then add the tomato mixture. Sprinkle over the Parmesan cheese and add the ricotta. Arrange the aubergine slices on top like a clock face then tuck the basil leaves under the slices.

8. Bake for 20 - 25 minutes until golden and bubbling. Serve hot.

TIP Sprinkling the aubergine slices with salt helps to extract their bitter juices.

Gorgonzola and artichoke pizza

This pizza is very versatile as it can be served hot, straight from the oven or cold for a picnic. Canned artichokes are a great storecupboard stand-by and a lot more convenient than cooking them from fresh. In this recipe I roast them before arranging them over mozzarella and Gorgonzola cheeses.

---

1 quantity of Pizza Dough (see page 12)

6 canned artichoke hearts

3 tablespoons olive oil

150 g (5 oz) mozzarella cheese

150 g (5 oz) Gorgonzola cheese

3 tablespoons freshly grated Parmesan cheese

1 tablespoon toasted pine kernels

1 teaspoon finely chopped fresh sage

sea salt and freshly ground black pepper

SERVES 4 – 6

1. Prepare the pizza dough as described on page 12.

2. Preheat the oven to 200C (400F/Gas 6). Rinse the artichoke hearts well, pat dry and put in a small roasting tin. Drizzle with the oil and roast in the oven for 10 minutes until golden.

3. Grate the mozzarella cheese and slice the Gorgonzola cheese. Cut the artichoke hearts into quarters.

4. On a very lightly floured surface, roll out the pizza dough very thinly into a round. Place on an oiled baking sheet.

5. Put the mozzarella cheese, Gorgonzola cheese and artichoke hearts on the pizza base. Sprinkle over the Parmesan cheese, pine kernels and sage and season with salt and pepper.

6. Bake in the oven for 20 - 25 minutes until golden and bubbling.

TIP Always rinse canned artichokes well to remove their saltiness.

Gorgonzola and artichoke pizza

Asparagus Calzone

Calzone is a folded pizza which preserves the flavours and makes the filling succulent. This is a real summertime recipe using asparagus when they are young, fresh and in season. By folding the dough over, you seal in the flavours and the smells until you cut into the Calzone.

½ quantity of Pizza Dough (see page 12)

2 tender young courgettes

sea salt and freshly ground black pepper

300 g (11 oz) fresh asparagus spears

150 g (5 oz) ricotta

1 tablespoon Parmesan cheese

2 tablespoons olive oil

SERVES 2

1. Prepare the pizza dough as described on page 12.

2. Slice the courgettes and put in a sieve. Sprinkle with salt and leave to drain for 20 minutes.

3. Meanwhile, trim the asparagus spears and put in a saucepan of boiling water. Return to the boil then drain and rinse under cold water. Cut into 5 cm (2 in) pieces. Rinse the courgette slices under cold water and pat dry with absorbent kitchen paper.

4. Put the asparagus, courgettes, ricotta and Parmesan cheese in a bowl and mix together. Season with salt and pepper to taste and stir in half the olive oil.

5. Preheat the oven to 200C (400F/Gas 6). On a very lightly floured surface, roll out the pizza dough into a 30 cm (12 in) round. Transfer to an oiled baking sheet.

6. Pile filling on one side, moisten the edge with water and pull the uncovered side over the filling. Using your fingers, seal the filling, fold the edges up and crimp.

7. Brush the Calzone with the remaining olive oil and bake in the oven for 20 - 25 minutes until golden brown. Allow to stand for 10 minutes before serving.

TIP If preferred, this recipe can be served as a pizza by simply spreading the filling over the entire dough round and not folding the dough over.

Shallot pizza

The marriage of the shallots and cheeses combine well to produce a delicious pizza. I like to roast the shallots in their skins which gives them a delicious, caramelised flavour. In Italy, they often boil the shallots and then skin them. You can use pickling onions instead of shallots although they have different flavours.

1 quantity of Pizza Dough (see page 12)

500 g (1 lb) shallots

250 g (8 oz) mozzarella cheese

75 g (3 oz) dolcelatte cheese

1 tablespoon olive oil

1 tablespoon balsamic vinegar

small handful of chopped fresh thyme

sea salt and freshly ground black pepper

S E R V E S   4 – 6

Illustrated in colour on page 2.

1. Prepare the pizza dough as described on page 12.

2. Preheat the oven to 200C (400F/Gas 6). Put the whole shallots in a roasting tin. Roast in the oven for 30 minutes, until they feel soft.

3. Meanwhile, grate the mozzarella cheese and slice the dolcelatte cheese. When cooked, skin the shallots and cut them into quarters.

4. On a very lightly floured surface, roll out the pizza dough very thinly into a round. Place on an oiled baking sheet.

5. Brush the pizza base with oil. Add the shallots and drizzle over the vinegar. Add the dolcelatte cheese then sprinkle over the mozzarella cheese and the thyme. Season with salt and pepper.

6. Bake in the oven for 20 minutes until golden and bubbling.

TIP For added flavour, the shallots can be skinned and quartered and then lightly fried in olive oil. Sprinkle with balsamic vinegar and leave overnight.

Mint pesto and aubergine pizza

This pizza has a byzantine flavour from Southern Italy, which I love. In Sicily, the cooking is very different in style to the rest of Italy. There is a hint of Greek and a lot of North African influence. The land is a rich and glorious terracotta colour and the sky a violent blue. This pizza captures that real Italian drama on a plate!

1 quantity of Pizza Dough (see page 12)

handful of chopped fresh mint, plus sprigs to garnish

50 g (2 oz) pine kernels

50 g (2 oz) freshly grated Parmesan cheese

1 small garlic clove

3 tablespoons olive oil

½ a small aubergine

sea salt and freshly ground black pepper

250 g (8 oz) mozzarella cheese

SERVES 4 – 6

Mint pesto and aubergine pizza

1. Prepare the pizza dough as described on page 12.

2. To make the Mint Pesto, put the mint, pine kernels, Parmesan cheese, garlic and 2 tablespoons oil in a mortar and using the pestle, grind until the mixture is a paste.

3. Slice the aubergine into thin rings. Put the slices in a colander, sprinkle with salt, cover and weigh down. Leave for about 30 minutes.

4. Rinse the aubergine slices and pat dry with absorbent kitchen paper. Heat the remaining 1 tablespoon oil in a frying pan and fry the aubergine slices until lightly golden on both sides.

5. Preheat the oven to 200C (400F/Gas 6). On a very lightly floured surface, roll out the pizza dough very thinly into a round. Place on an oiled baking sheet.

6. Slice the mozzarella cheese. Spread a generous layer of mint pesto on to the pizza base, then arrange the mozzarella and aubergine slices on top. Season with salt and pepper and add the remaining mint pesto. Bake in the oven for 20 minutes until golden and bubbling. Serve garnished with sprigs of mint.

TIP If you do not have a pestle and mortar you can prepare the mint pesto in a food processor or blender. Simply blend the ingredients together until very creamy.

Pizza with four cheeses

The combination of the four cheeses produces a delicious pizza. Although it comes from Switzerland, the Italians love Gruyère and it is traditional to use it in this classic pizza.

1 quantity of Pizza Dough (see page 12)

100 g (4 oz) mozzarella cheese

100 g (4 oz) Gruyère cheese

100 g (4 oz) Gorgonzola cheese

handful of fresh basil leaves, torn

50 g (2 oz) piece of fresh Parmesan cheese

freshly ground black pepper

SERVES 4 – 6

1. Prepare the pizza dough as described on page 12.

2. Preheat the oven to 200C (400F/Gas 6). On a very lightly floured surface, roll out the dough very thinly into a round. Place on an oiled baking sheet.

3. Slice the mozzarella, Gruyère and Gorgonzola cheese. Spread the basil leaves over the pizza dough base. Arrange the sliced cheeses on top. Using a potato peeler, shave over the Parmesan cheese. Add a generous sprinkling of pepper.

4. Bake in the oven for 20 - 25 minutes until golden and bubbling.

Tomato pizza

This is probably the most simple pizza of all and the one that I could almost say is my favourite. I love simple food. Good ingredients, blended carefully together and used at their freshest are a joy. For the best flavour, choose bright red, ripe tomatoes and smell their stalk end. The best tomatoes have a strong peppery aroma.

1 quantity of Pizza Dough (see page 12)

625 g (1¼ lb) cherry tomatoes

250 g (8 oz) mozzarella cheese

large handful of fresh basil leaves, torn

small handful of fresh oregano, chopped

sea salt and freshly ground black pepper

SERVES 4 – 6

1. Prepare the pizza dough as described on page 12.

2. Cut the tomatoes in half. Grate the mozzarella cheese.

3. Preheat the oven to 200C (400F/Gas 6). On a very lightly floured surface, roll out the dough very thinly into a round. Place on an oiled baking sheet.

4. Spread the basil leaves over the pizza base then add the tomato halves, oregano, salt, pepper and mozzarella cheese.

5. Bake in the oven for about 20 minutes until the tomatoes are softened and the cheese bubbling and golden.

Pizza with courgette flowers

I ate this Pizza in Rome when my plane had been delayed for three hours. At the time I was very put out by the inconvenience but with hindsight I was lucky otherwise I would never have had the opportunity to enjoy it. You can buy courgettes with their flowers on them in quality and specialist vegetable shops over here – but in every market in Italy.

---

1 quantity of Pizza Dough (see page 12)

225 g (8 oz) mozzarella cheese

75 g (3 oz) Gruyère cheese

8 courgette flowers

handful of fresh basil leaves, torn

1 teaspoon chopped fresh oregano

freshly ground black pepper

SERVES 4 – 6

1. Prepare the pizza dough as described on page 12.

2. Thinly slice the mozzarella cheese. Grate the Gruyère cheese. Cut the courgette flowers in half.

3. Preheat the oven to 200C (400F/Gas 6). On a very lightly floured surface, roll out the dough very thinly into a round. Place on an oiled baking sheet.

4. To assemble the pizza, lay the basil over the pizza base and sprinkle over the oregano. Add the mozzarella and Gruyère cheese and then the courgette flowers. Season with pepper.

5. Bake in the oven for 20 minutes until golden and bubbling. Serve the pizza immediately.

TIP Courgettes are extremely easy to grow in the garden and you can then make use of the flowers on a pizza. Just one grow bag, 3 seeds, some sun and lots of water are all you need.

Pizza Norcina

I first enjoyed this pizza in Norcina, in Umbria, which is famous for truffles. It was so good that I returned the following day for another. I have been truffle hunting in Umbria – all dressed up in hunting gear. It is a real occasion and taken very seriously. To get a good truffle is a real prize and it becomes a talking point for months on end.

1 quantity of Pizza Dough (see page 12)

200 g (7 oz) dried sliced porcini mushrooms or a combination of porcini and fresh flat mushrooms

250 g (8 oz) mozzarella cheese

2 tablespoons olive oil

1 garlic clove, crushed

sea salt and freshly ground black pepper

25 g (1 oz) truffle condiment

SERVES 4 – 6

1. Prepare the pizza dough as described on page 12.

2. Soak the porcini in warm water for about 20 minutes to reconstitute. Slice the fresh mushrooms. Grate the mozzarella cheese.

3. Drain the porcini and pat dry. Heat the oil in a medium frying pan, add the porcini and fresh mushrooms and fry until softened. Add the garlic, salt and pepper.

4. Preheat the oven to 200C (400F/Gas 6). On a very lightly floured surface, roll out the pizza dough very thinly into a round. Place on an oiled baking sheet.

5. Top the pizza base with the mushrooms and cheese then add little mounds of truffle condiment.

6. Bake in the oven for 20 - 25 minutes until golden and bubbling. Serve immediately.

TIP Truffle condiment, sold in jars, is available in good delicatessens. It is expensive so this pizza is for special occasions.

Pizza Norcina

Pizza with goats' cheese, thyme and walnut oil

I usually buy a wedge of a hard goats' cheese from a local deli with a good turnover but I sometimes get the round, soft, pre-packed ones from the supermarket. The garlic is simmered in water until it is soft which makes the flavour more subtle.

1 quantity of Pizza Dough (see page 12)

4 garlic cloves

4, preferably plum, tomatoes

175 g (6 oz) soft goats' cheese

50 g (2 oz) pine kernels

3 tablespoons walnut oil

sea salt and freshly ground black pepper

handful of fresh thyme, chopped

SERVES 4 – 6

1. Prepare the pizza dough as described on page 12.

2. Put the garlic cloves in a small saucepan, cover with water and simmer for 10 - 15 minutes, until soft.

3. Meanwhile, slice the tomatoes and goats' cheese. Toast the pine kernels on a sheet of foil under the grill, turning them frequently. When the garlic cloves are soft, drain and, using a fork, mash into a purée.

4. Preheat the oven to 200C (400F/Gas 6). On a very lightly floured surface, roll out the pizza dough very thinly into a round. Place on an oiled baking sheet.

5. Sprinkle the rolled out dough with half of the walnut oil. Arrange the sliced tomatoes on the pizza and dot with the garlic purée. Arrange the cheese slices on top. Sprinkle with salt, pepper, the remaining oil and the pine kernels.

6. Bake in the oven for 20 - 25 minutes until golden and bubbling. Serve sprinkled with chopped thyme.

TIP Italian Taleggio cheese is good instead of the goats' cheese.

Folded onion pizza

I really like this recipe from my friends in Apulia on the east coast of Italy. Apulia has a Greek influence in its food and very hot summers. This pizza is a memorable blend of salty olives, plump raisins and sweet, golden onions. It's ideal for lunch served with a fresh green salad.

1 quantity of Pizza Dough (see page 12)

625 g (1¼ lb) red onions

150 g (5 oz) stoned black olives

4 tomatoes

100 g (4 oz) raisins

4 tablespoons olive oil

50 g (2 oz) freshly grated Parmesan cheese

50 g (2 oz) freshly grated pecorino cheese

sea salt and freshly ground black pepper

SERVES 4 – 6

1. Prepare the pizza dough as described on page 12.

2. Slice the onions. Finely chop the olives. Put tomatoes in a bowl, cover with boiling water for about 40 seconds then plunge into cold water. Skin then chop the flesh.

3. Soak the raisins in lukewarm water for 15 minutes. Meanwhile, heat 2 tablespoons of oil in a saucepan, add onions and fry until golden. Add olives and tomatoes. Drain and dry the raisins then add to mixture. Cook for a further 10 minutes.

4. Remove the pan from the heat and stir in the Parmesan and pecorino cheese. Season with salt and pepper to taste.

5. Divide the pizza dough into two pieces. On a very lightly floured surface, roll out each piece of dough to a 23 cm (9 in) round. Spread the filling over one half of dough and place the second half on top. Press the edges together to seal.

6. Place on an oiled baking sheet and leave to rise for 30 minutes.

7. Preheat the oven to 200C (400F/Gas 6). Brush the pizza with the remaining oil then bake for 15 minutes. Lower the temperature to 190C (375F/Gas 5) and cook for a further 25 minutes. Serve warm.

TIP The best way to chop onions and avoid crying is to keep the root intact for as long as possible as it is this that, when cut, releases an acid which makes us cry.

Focaccia

Focaccia is a large flat oval bread which is eaten all over Italy in many different guises and with just as many names. It can be topped or filled with a variety of ingredients and can be thick, thin, soft or crisp. A good focaccia is essentially an olive oil dough, flavoured with salt, rosemary and garlic on top. When you bite into the dough, the oil should dribble down your chin. This is my basic recipe for focaccia and the ones that follow include a filling.

---

15 g (½ oz) fresh yeast or 1½ teaspoons dried yeast and a pinch of sugar

275 ml (9 fl oz) hand-hot water

500 g (1 lb) strong white unbleached flour, preferably 'O' grade

3 teaspoons coarse sea salt

4 tablespoons olive oil, plus extra to drizzle on top

2 garlic cloves, finely chopped

1 medium sprig of rosemary, chopped

SERVES 4 – 6

1. Cream the fresh yeast with 1 tablespoon of the hand-hot water. (If using dried yeast, sprinkle it into 1 tablespoon of the hand-hot water with the sugar and leave in a warm place for 15 minutes until frothy).

2. Put the flour and 1 teaspoon salt in a large bowl and mix well together. Make a reservoir in the centre and pour in the yeast liquid, 3 tablespoons of the oil and some of the water. Mix together, gradually adding the water, to form a soft dough

3. Turn the dough on to a work surface and knead vigorously for 10 minutes, to form a smooth dough.

4. Return dough to a bowl, cover with a tea-towel and leave in a warm place for about 45 minutes until doubled in size.

5. When dough has risen, knead again for 1 - 2 minutes to knock out the air bubbles.

6. On a lightly floured surface, roll out the dough to an oval about 33 cm (13 in) long. Place on an oiled baking sheet and leave to rise in a warm place, for 20 - 30 minutes, until doubled in size.

7. Preheat the oven to 200C (400F/Gas 6). Using your fingertips, dimple the surface of the dough and drizzle on the remaining oil. Sprinkle with the remaining salt, the garlic and rosemary. Transfer the Focaccia to a hot baking sheet, terracotta pizza stone or some clean oiled bricks in your oven and bake for 20 - 25 minutes, until golden. Drizzle with more oil and cool on a wire rack.

Focaccia

Spinach, olive and onion focaccia

I first enjoyed this focaccia in Napoli airport. The olive oil dough has a filling baked in the middle of it. It is made as a large, flat round and cut into wedges to serve. Peperoncini are tiny, long, thin chillies. You don't need much to pep up a dish and they last for a year or two. I make this to take on picnics.

DOUGH

15 g (½ oz) fresh yeast or 1½ teaspoons dried yeast and a pinch of sugar

275 ml (9 fl oz) hand-hot water

500 g (1 lb) strong white unbleached flour, preferably 'O' grade

1 teaspoon sea salt

3 tablespoons olive oil

FILLING

1 large red onion

750 g (1½ lb) fresh spinach

75 g (3 oz) mozzarella cheese

3 tablespoons olive oil

1 garlic clove, crushed

½ a dried peperoncini, crushed

125 g (4 oz) stoned green olives

sea salt and freshly ground black pepper

SERVES 4 – 6

1. Prepare the focaccia dough up to step 6 as described on page 31.

2. Skin and slice the onion. Finely chop the spinach. Chop the mozzarella cheese.

3. Heat 2 tablespoons of the olive oil in a large frying pan, add the onion, garlic and peperoncini and cook for 5 minutes until soft. Add the spinach and olives and cook over a medium heat until the spinach wilts. Remove from the heat and add the mozzarella cheese. Season with salt and pepper.

4. Divide the dough into 2 pieces. On a lightly floured surface, roll out each piece of dough to a thin 33 cm (13 in) round. Place one round on an oiled baking sheet.

5. Spread the filling over the round. Dampen the edge and cover with the second round of dough. Pinch the edges together to seal and, using your fingertips, dimple the surface.

6. Leave to rise in a warm place for 30 minutes, until doubled in size.

7. Preheat the oven to 200C (400F/Gas 6). Drizzle the remaining tablespoon of olive oil over the dough and sprinkle with salt. Transfer the dough to a hot baking sheet, terracotta pizza stone or bricks and bake in the oven for 25 minutes until golden. Leave to cool slightly on a wire rack then serve warm.

TIP Always use fresh spinach in this recipe. Wash it well and if the stalks are tough, remove them.

Ricotta focaccia with basil

This focaccia has a layer of ricotta and basil sandwiched in the middle. It makes a great accompaniment to a bowl of broth, a salad or on its own as a change from a sandwich. Ricotta is made from the whey left over from making Parmesan. If you can buy it fresh from a deli then you'll find that it has a better flavour than a processed, pre-packed version.

DOUGH

15 g (½ oz) fresh yeast or 1½ teaspoons dried yeast and a pinch of sugar

275 ml (9 fl oz) hand-hot water

500 g (1 lb) strong white unbleached flour, preferably 'O' grade

1 teaspoon sea salt

3 tablespoons olive oil

FILLING

250 g (8 oz) ricotta

handful of fresh basil leaves, torn

3 tablespoons olive oil

coarse sea salt and freshly ground black pepper

SERVES 4 – 6

1. Prepare the focaccia dough up to step 6 as described on page 31.

2. Divide the dough into 2 pieces. On a lightly floured surface, roll out each piece of dough to a 33 cm (13 in) round. Place one round on an oiled baking sheet.

3. Spread the ricotta over the round. Add the basil, 1 tablespoon of olive oil, salt and pepper. Dampen the edge and cover with the second round of dough. Pinch the edges together to seal and, using your fingertips, dimple the surface.

4. Leave to rise in a warm place for 30 minutes, until doubled in size.

5. Preheat the oven to 200C (400F/Gas 6). Drizzle 1 tablespoon of olive oil over the Focaccia and sprinkle with salt. Transfer the Focaccia to a hot baking sheet, terracotta pizza stone or bricks and bake in the oven for 25 minutes until golden. Drizzle over the remaining olive oil. Leave to cool slightly on a wire rack then serve warm.

TIP Tear basil, as opposed to cutting it, so as not to ruin its delicate flavour.

Tomato, onion and rocket focaccia

This focaccia with its thumbprint top has a moist, herb-scented middle. Make sure you pinch the edges of the dough well to seal in the filling.

DOUGH

15 g (½ oz) fresh yeast or 1½ teaspoons dried yeast and a pinch of sugar

275 ml (9 fl oz) hand-hot water

500 g (1 lb) strong white unbleached flour, preferably 'O' grade

1 teaspoon sea salt

3 tablespoons olive oil

FILLING

450 g (1 lb) cherry tomatoes

2 red onions

3 tablespoons olive oil

coarse sea salt and freshly ground black pepper

175 g (6 oz) mozzarella cheese

1½ handfuls of rocket

3 teaspoons finely chopped fresh oregano

SERVES 4 – 6

1. Prepare the focaccia dough up to step 6 as described on page 31.

2. Preheat the oven to 200C (400F/Gas 6). Put the whole tomatoes in a roasting tin (without oil) and roast for 20 minutes.

3. Meanwhile, skin and roughly chop the onions. Heat 1 tablespoon oil in a frying pan, add the onions and fry for about 5 minutes until softened. Season with salt and pepper. Chop the mozzarella cheese.

4. Divide the dough into 2 pieces. On a lightly floured surface, roll out each piece of dough to a thin 33 cm (13 in) round. Place one round on an oiled baking sheet.

5. Spread the onions over the round. Add the tomatoes and then the cheese. Sprinkle with rocket and oregano. Dampen the edge and cover with the second round of dough. Pinch the edges together and, using your fingertips, dimple the surface.

6. Leave to rise in a warm place for 30 minutes, until doubled in size.

7. Drizzle over the remaining oil and sprinkle with salt. Transfer dough to a hot baking sheet, pizza stone or bricks and bake for 25 minutes until golden. Serve warm.

TIP Rocket can be grown very easily in the garden. It grows like a weed and in 6 weeks you can harvest your own tender, green leaves. Be warned – it is an aphrodisiac and very addictive!

Tomato, onion and rocket focaccia

Focaccia with oil and sage

This Focaccia has a light, open texture, is scented with sage and has a delicate taste. You will find you cannot stop eating it!

DOUGH

15 g (½ oz) fresh yeast or 1½ teaspoons dried yeast and a pinch of sugar

275 ml (9 fl oz) hand-hot water

525 g (18 oz) strong white unbleached flour, preferably 'O' grade

75 ml (3 fl oz) dry white wine

75 ml (3 fl oz) light olive oil

20 fresh sage leaves, chopped

1 tablespoon sea salt

2 oz (50 g) freshly grated Parmesan cheese

TO FINISH

2 tablespoons well-flavoured olive oil

1 - 2 teaspoons coarse sea salt

2 fresh sage leaves, chopped

SERVES 4 – 6

1. In a large bowl, cream the fresh yeast with 150 ml (¼ pint) of the water. (If using dried yeast, sprinkle it into 150 ml (¼ pint) of the water with the sugar and leave in a warm place for 15 minutes until frothy.)

2. Stir 150 g (5 oz) flour into the yeast liquid and beat until smooth. Cover the bowl tightly and leave to rise in a warm place for about 30 minutes.

3. Add the remaining 125 ml (4 fl oz) water, the wine, oil, sage, salt and cheese to the sponge mixture. Gradually whisk in the remaining flour until the dough is very soft and sticky.

4. On a lightly floured surface, knead the dough for 10 minutes, adding more flour if necessary. It should be soft but not wet.

5. Place dough in a lightly oiled bowl, cover and leave in a warm place for 1 hour.

6. When risen, knead again for 1 - 2 minutes. Roll out to a 33 cm (13 in) round. Place on an oiled baking sheet, cover and leave for 1 hour.

7. Preheat the oven to 200C (400F/Gas 6). Dimple the top of the Focaccia, drizzle over oil and sprinkle with salt and sage. Bake for 25 - 30 minutes until golden. Leave to cool.

TIP If more convenient, you can leave the dough to rise in the fridge overnight. Allow it to return to room temperature, for about 1 hour, before shaping.

Flat bread with olives

This is quite a special bread eaten all over Italy. The addition of dry white wine makes the focaccia rich and delicious. The dough has olives kneaded through it plus some baked on the top. It is wonderful on its own or with cheeses and salad, for a light summer's lunch.

---

50 g (2 oz) fresh yeast or 25 g (1 oz) dried yeast and 1 teaspoon sugar

350 ml (12 fl oz) hand-hot water

400 g (14 oz) stoned black olives, preserved in oil

1 kg (2 lb) strong white unbleached flour, preferably 'O' grade

sea salt

150 ml (¼ pint) olive oil, plus extra for brushing

150 ml (¼ pint) dry white wine

1 tablespoon chopped fresh thyme

2 tablespoons chopped fresh oregano

SERVES 8

1. Cream the fresh yeast with 150 ml (¼ pint) of the water. (If using dried yeast, sprinkle it into 150 ml (¼ pint) of the water with the sugar and leave in a warm place for 15 minutes until frothy. Chop the olives.

2. Mix the flour and 1 teaspoon salt together. Add the liquid yeast, oil, wine and some of the water. Mix together, gradually adding more water, to form a dough. Work in two-thirds of the olives and all the thyme.

3. Turn the dough on to a work surface and knead well for 10 minutes. Return the dough to a bowl, cover with a tea-towel and leave in a warm place for about 1½ hours until doubled in size.

4. When dough has risen, knead again for 1 - 2 minutes to knock out the air bubbles.

5. Roll out the dough to a 1 cm (½ in) thick round. Place on an oiled baking sheet.

6. Sprinkle with salt, the oregano and remaining olives. Using your fingertips, make dimples all over the surface.

7. Leave to rise in a warm place for 30 minutes until doubled in size.

8. Preheat the oven to 220C (425F/Gas 7). Brush the bread generously with olive oil. Bake in the oven for 25 minutes until golden. Brush with oil and serve hot.

TIP Don't skimp on the olives as they make the world of difference.

Pitta

This is a yeasted pie from Calabria, Southern Italy. My recipe is filled with cheese and peppers but ham or bacon is another popular filling. I've suggested caciocavallo cheese but if you are unable to buy it, you could use provolone cheese or extra ricotta.

DOUGH

15 g (½ oz) fresh yeast or 1½ teaspoons dried yeast and a pinch of sugar

6 tablespoons hand-hot water

300 g (11 oz) strong white unbleached flour, preferably 'O' grade

sea salt

2 eggs

20 g (¾ oz) butter

1 tablespoon olive oil

FILLING

2 red peppers

100 g (4 oz) caciocavallo cheese

2 eggs, hard-boiled

sea salt and freshly ground black pepper

200 g (7 oz) ricotta

SERVES 6

Pitta

1. To make the dough, cream the fresh yeast with 4 tablespoons of the water. (If using dried yeast, sprinkle it into 4 tablespoons water with the sugar and leave in a warm place for 15 minutes until frothy).

2. Sift half of the flour and a pinch of salt together. Make a reservoir in the centre, add the yeast liquid and remaining water and mix well to form a smooth dough. Shape into a ball and leave to rise in a warm place for 1 hour.

3. Preheat the oven to 200C (400F/Gas 6). Put the peppers on a baking sheet and roast for 20 minutes until deflated and slightly charred, turning. Leave to cool then skin and roughly chop the flesh. Slice the caciocavallo cheese and hard-boiled eggs.

4. When the dough has risen, beat the eggs together and melt the butter. Sift the remaining flour on to a work surface and work into the risen dough with the eggs, butter and oil. Knead until smooth.

5. On a lightly floured surface, roll out two-thirds of the dough to a 28 cm (11 in) round. Use to line a 23 cm (9 in) cake tin, letting it come slightly up the sides. Arrange cheese, egg slices sprinkled with salt and pepper, ricotta and peppers in the tin.

6. Roll out remaining dough to make a lid. Place round over the filling. Fold edges inwards, pressing together to seal. Leave to rise in a warm place for 30 minutes.

7. Preheat the oven to 200C (400F/Gas 6). Brush the top of the pie with oil. Bake for 30 minutes until golden. Serve warm.

Potato pizza

This, although you may think it sounds heavy, is deliciously light and tasty. This is for my father – a great potato lover – who is responsible for my mother spending half her life at the sink, peeling and preparing potatoes. Flavoured with cheeses and nutmeg, this is great with a glass of red wine and a salad for a simple supper.

275 g (10 oz) potatoes (see Tip)

50 g (2 oz) mozzarella cheese

50 g (2 oz) freshly grated Parmesan cheese

pinch of freshly grated nutmeg

sea salt and freshly ground black pepper

15 g (½ oz) fresh yeast or 1½ teaspoons dried yeast and a pinch of sugar

450 ml (¾ pint) hand-hot water

900 g (2 lb) strong white unbleached flour, preferably 'O' grade

2 tablespoons olive oil

SERVES 4 – 6

1. Cook the potatoes in their skins in boiling water for about 20 minutes until tender. Drain then, as soon as they are cool enough to handle, peel and mash well. Grate the mozzarella cheese and add to the potatoes with the Parmesan cheese, nutmeg, 2 teaspoons salt and 1 teaspoon pepper. Mix well together.

2. Cream the fresh yeast with 150 ml (¼ pint) of the water. (If using dried yeast, sprinkle it into 150 ml (¼ pint) water with the sugar and leave in a warm place for 15 minutes until frothy).

3. Spread the mashed potato on to the work surface, then sprinkle with the flour. Add the yeast liquid and mix together with enough of the remaining water to form a smooth dough. Knead for about 5 minutes.

4. Place the dough on an oiled baking sheet, flatten with a rolling pin and roll out to form a 25 cm (10 in) round.

5. Cover with a clean tea-towel and leave to rise in a warm place for about 1½ hours until doubled in size.

6. Preheat the oven to 200C (400F/Gas 6). Brush the dough with the oil and bake in the oven for 40 minutes or until golden. Leave to cool slightly before serving warm.

TIP I think the best types of potatoes to use for this pizza are Desiree or Pentland Crown as they mash well.

Flat bread with grapes

This is a sweet pizza and is typical of Tuscany, where I first enjoyed it. Sometimes it has fennel seeds sprinkled over the top and, served with a dollop of mascarpone on the side, it is the Italian equivalent of an English Cream Tea. It is also good as a snack, served with a glass of wine or even cheese.

---

200 g (7 oz) raisins

1 wine glass of Vin Santo or a sweet dessert wine

150 ml (¼ pint) milk

7 g (¼ oz) fresh yeast or 1 teaspoon dried yeast

350 g (12 oz) strong white unbleached flour, preferably 'O' grade

pinch of sea salt

75 g (3 oz) golden caster sugar

500 g (1 lb) black grapes, seeded

SERVES 4 – 6

1. Put the raisins in a bowl, pour over the wine and leave to soak for at least 2 hours.

2. Gently warm the milk. Cream the fresh yeast with the milk. (If using dried yeast, sprinkle it into the milk and leave in a warm place for 15 minutes until frothy).

3. In a large bowl, mix together the flour, salt and 50 g (2 oz) of the sugar. Add the yeast liquid and mix to form a soft dough.

4. Turn the dough on to a work surface and knead for 10 minutes until smooth. Put in a bowl, cover with a tea-towel and leave in a warm place for 1 hour, until doubled in size.

5. When the dough has risen, knead again for 1 - 2 minutes. Drain the raisins.

6. Divide the dough into 2 pieces. Roll out each piece to a 20 cm (8 in) round. Place one round on a floured baking sheet.

7. Cover the round with half of the grapes and half of the drained raisins. Dampen the edge, cover with the second round and seal. Top with the remaining grapes and raisins.

8. Leave to rise in a warm place for about 20 minutes until doubled in size.

9. Preheat the oven to 180C (350F/Gas 4). Sprinkle the dough with the remaining sugar. Bake for about 45 minutes until golden. Cool slightly before serving warm.

TIP You could use red grapes in this recipe when in season, usually around September.

Pasta

PASTA is the soul of Italian life. Like pizza, it should be made from strong flour, rich in gluten. It is the gluten that gives pasta its true texture. The wheat is very finely milled to produce 'OO' grade flour which is soft and silky. It is available from good delicatessens and specialist Italian shops. Plain white flour may be used but the pasta will be softer.

Pasta is made in hundreds of different shapes, each one with a different clinging ability to the all-important sauce. The simple rule of thumb is that hollow or twisted shapes take chunky sauces and that the flatter the pasta the richer the sauce.

Pasta fresca (fresh pasta) that is vacuum sealed can be limp and tasteless but Italian food shops that make pasta on the premises sell something nearer to the real thing. Pasta secca (dried pasta) is good, however, the ultimate pasta is home-made.

SERVING PASTA

Italians almost always serve pasta as a course on its own after the antipasto and before the main course. It is served in a deep plate which prevents the sauce from splashing and helps to keep the pasta warm. The pasta is never served in a huge mound.

AMOUNTS TO SERVE

DRIED PASTA
75 - 100 g (3 - 4 oz) per person

FRESH PASTA
100 - 150 g (4 - 5 oz) per person

FILLED PASTA
175 - 200 g (6 - 7 oz) per person

EATING PASTA

With a fork only please. Use the fork to lift the pasta and sauce together. Make a small space at the side of your plate and twist.

Home-made pasta dough

200 g (7 oz) strong white unbleached flour, preferably 'OO' grade

sea salt

2 large eggs, preferably free range

1 tablespoon olive oil

semolina, for sprinkling

SERVES 2

TIP You may like to make double the quantity of pasta dough and either freeze any leftover dough or store it in the fridge, well wrapped, for up to 3 days.

1. Sift the flour into a large bowl or into a mound on to a work surface and make a well in the centre. Add a pinch of salt, the eggs and the oil.

2. Using a fork at first and then your hands, draw in the flour from the inside of the well, gradually adding more flour until the mixture resembles a coarse dough. This is when I would add some water. I can't say how much, but a little to make the paste more pliable.

3. Now the part of pasta making I enjoy the most: standing with one foot in front of the other, knead the dough by pushing the paste away from you with the heel of your hand and give the paste a quarter turn. Repeat this process for about 10 minutes until you have a smooth, firm, soft dough.

4. Put the dough in a polythene bag and leave to rest in the fridge for 30 minutes. (During this time, the sauce can be made).

Rolling and cooking pasta

Dividing dough into manageable pieces before rolling out.

1. Put the pasta, a small piece at a time, into a pasta machine and roll out. Repeat with the remaining dough. Alternatively, using a long, thin rolling pin and a little flour, roll out the dough as thinly as possible.

2. Carefully transfer the sheet of dough to a clean tea-towel and leave for 10 minutes to dry a little before cutting – I like to sprinkle a little semolina or flour over the pasta to help in the drying process.

3. Place dough in the attachment of the machine and cut into the required shape. Alternatively, using a sharp knife or pastry wheel, cut the sheets of pasta into the required shape. To cut tagliatelle, fold the pasta sheet into a flat roll about 8 cm (3 in) wide then cut into 1 cm (½ in) wide strips. Spread the cut pasta out on to a clean tea-towel and leave to dry for a minimum of 10 minutes. Use within 3 days.

4. To cook: bring a large, deep saucepan of water to the boil (allow 1 litre (1³/4 pints) to 100 g (4 oz) pasta). Add the pasta, return to the boil then cook for 4 minutes until just tender. (Allow an extra 2 minutes if cooking from frozen).

5. Drain the pasta in a colander and shake well to remove excess liquid. Serve immediately, tossed in a knob of butter, 1 tablespoon olive oil, with a sauce or according to individual recipes.

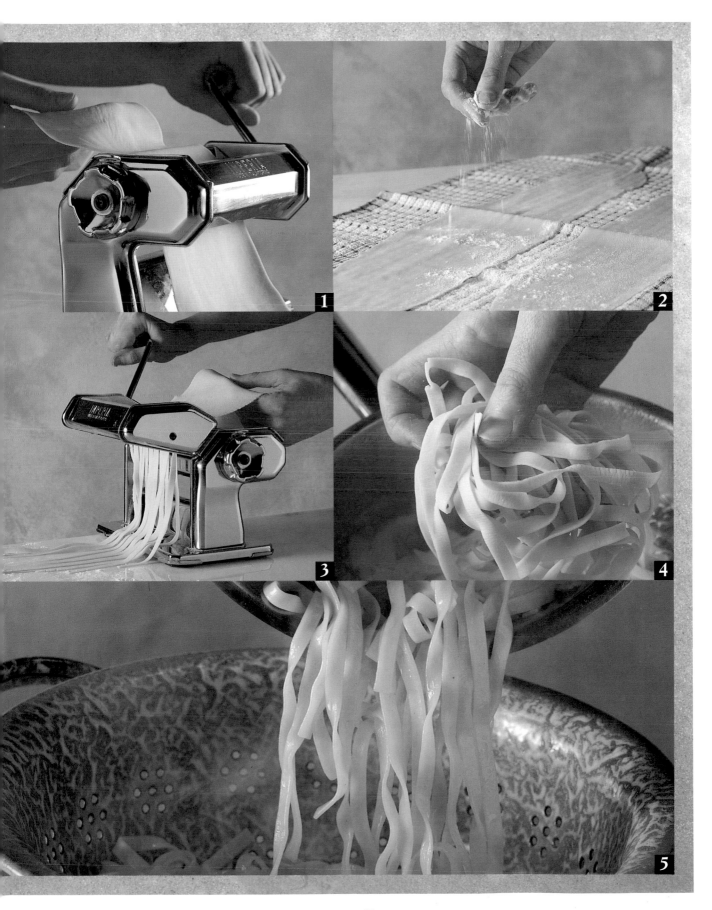

Shapes

There are hunderds of different shapes of fresh and dried pasta. They may even be coloured, for example green or red, which means spinach or tomato has been added to the dough.
A selection of available pasta shapes are illustrated, although some may have a different name in Italy, where the different regions have their own pasta names and shapes.

Below: Fresh pasta – 1. Tomato, plain and spinach tagliatelle 2. Spaghetti 3. Small tortellini 4. Large tortellini 5. Plain ravioli 6. Plain and spinach tagliarini 7. Tomato fusilli 8. Tomato ravioli.
Right: Dried pasta – 1. Ziti 2. Orecchiette 3. Penne 4. Fettuccine 5. Spinach fettuccine 6. Tagliatelle

7. Spinach tagliatelle
8. Papardelle 9. Vermicelli
10. Casarecce 11. Rigatoni
12. Campanelle 13. Two sizes of conchiglie 14. Fiochette
15.Diti-small macaroni
16. Farfalle 17. Anellini
18. Mafaldini 19. Lasagne
20. Cannelloni
21. Spaghetti.

Gorgonzola and pine kernels with rigatoni

This dish was born by accident just from leftovers and I hope it will become popular with your friends and family, as it has with mine. Mountain Gorgonzola is the best and the bluest. It melts to a smooth and creamy sauce which is perfect with the broccoli and cauliflower.

40 g (1½ oz) pine kernels

65 g (2½ oz) broccoli florets

65 g (2½ oz) cauliflower florets

1 red onion

2 tablespoon olive oil

1 teaspoon chopped fresh thyme

sea salt and freshly ground black pepper

200 g (7 oz) rigatoni (ridged, broad tube pasta)

100 g (4 oz) Gorgonzola cheese

SERVES 2

Illustrated in colour on page 42

1. Toast the pine kernels on a sheet of foil under the grill, turning them frequently.

2. Steam the broccoli and cauliflower florets for about 8 minutes, depending on size, until tender.

3. Meanwhile, skin and finely chop the onion. Heat the oil in a saucepan and fry the onion until softened. Add the thyme, salt and pepper.

4. Cook the pasta in a large saucepan of boiling salted water for 12 minutes until just tender.

5. Cut the cheese into cubes and add to the onions, along with the nuts, broccoli and cauliflower. Drain the pasta and toss into the vegetables. Adjust seasonings to taste and serve.

TIP Fusilli, which are spiral-shaped pasta, are equally good in this recipe and 250 g (8 oz) cooked spinach could be used instead of the broccoli and cauliflower.

Pasta with turnip tops

I have Mario and Luisa who live in Apulia, southern Italy to thank for this recipe. They are very old family friends in the fruit business. This dish is as typical to the region as Yorkshire Pudding is to Yorkshire, and is served in every trattoria. It is made from the leafy green tops of new turnips as they come in to season.

300 g (11 oz) turnip tops (see Tip)

3 tomatoes

175 g (6 oz) orecchietti (little pasta ears)

sea salt and freshly ground black pepper

2 tablespoons olive oil

1 garlic clove, sliced

1 small dried peperoncino, finely chopped (optional)

freshly grated pecorino cheese

SERVES 2

Illustrated in colour on page 52

1. Wash the turnip tops well. Steam or boil for about 8 minutes until tender.

2. Put the tomatoes in a bowl, cover with boiling water for about 40 seconds then plunge into cold water. Using a sharp knife, peel off the skins then chop the flesh, discarding the seeds.

3. Cook the pasta in a large saucepan of boiling salted water for about 20 minutes until just tender.

4. Put the oil and garlic in a pan and fry until beginning to colour. Add the tomatoes and peperoncino, if using.

5. Drain the pasta and add the turnip tops and tomato mixture and mix well. Serve with grated cheese.

TIP Turnip tops are the green, sprouting part of turnips. If they are not available, you can use Swiss chard, spinach or kale or even spring cabbage, which should be roughly torn then steamed or boiled until tender.

Pappardelle with truffles and porcini

I first ate this dish in Umbria, famous for both truffles and porcini. It was so good, I could not stop eating it.

50 g (2 oz) dried sliced porcini

200 g (7 oz) pappardelle (long broad pasta)

sea salt and freshly ground black pepper

1 tablespoon olive oil

1 garlic clove, crushed

50 g (2 oz) truffle condiment

2 tablespoons mascarpone cheese

1 tablespoon dry white wine

shavings of Parmesan cheese, to serve

SERVES 2

1. Soak the porcini in water for 20 minutes then drain.

2. Cook the pasta in boiling salted water for 12 minutes until just tender.

3. Meanwhile, heat the oil in a pan, add the garlic, truffle condiment and porcini and cook gently for 10 minutes. Add the mascarpone cheese, wine, salt and pepper.

4. Drain the pasta and toss in the truffle and porcini mixture. Serve with Parmesan.

TIP The flavour of truffle condiment is very concentrated so that although it is expensive, you don't need much.

Spaghetti with cheese and pepper

This is the simplest recipe of all and is therefore dedicated to tired cooks!

200 g (7 oz) spaghetti

sea salt

little knob of unsalted butter

50 g (2 oz) freshly grated Parmesan cheese

½ teaspoon freshly ground black pepper

SERVES 2

1. Cook the spaghetti in a large saucepan of boiling salted water for about 10 minutes until just tender.

2. Drain the pasta and add the butter, cheese and pepper. Stir well and serve straight away. It couldn't be simpler.

TIP If spaghetti and Parmesan cheese are always in your store cupboard, this dish can be prepared at any time.

Top: Pappardelle with truffles and porcini.

Bottom: Pasta with turnip tops (see page 51)

Pasta with garlic and oil

This is another utterly simple dish, popular all over Italy. Be warned – eat in couples, because of the garlic!

200 g (7 oz) spaghetti

sea salt

2 garlic cloves, crushed

½ small fresh red chilli, seeded and finely chopped, or 1 small dried peperoncino, crushed

65 ml (2½ oz) fruity or lemony extra virgin olive oil

handful of flat-leaved parsley, finely chopped

SERVES 2

1. Cook the pasta in boiling salted water for about 10 minutes until just tender.

2. Meanwhile, beat the garlic, chilli pepper and a pinch of salt into the olive oil.

3. When the pasta is cooked, drain and quickly dress with the oil mixture. Serve sprinkled generously with the parsley.

TIP To mask the smell of garlic try; a glass of milk, a handful of parsley, an apple, a strong expresso coffee or a measure of Campari.

Spaghetti with tiny tomatoes

This is a typical dish from Naples.

500 g (1 lb) cherry tomatoes

3 large garlic cloves, cut into slithers

sea salt and freshly ground black pepper

200 g (7 oz) spaghetti

1 small hot chilli pepper, seeded and chopped (optional)

1 tablespoon olive oil (if necessary)

handful of fresh basil, torn

2 tablespoons extra virgin olive oil

freshly grated Parmesan cheese, to serve

SERVES 2

1. Preheat the oven to 150C (300F/Gas 2). Cut the tomatoes in half and place on a baking sheet. Place a slither of garlic on top and a little sprinkling of salt. Bake for 1¼ hours until dry but still squashy.

2. Cook the pasta in boiling salted water for about 10 minutes until just tender. If using chilli, fry in olive oil to just colour then remove from heat.

3. Drain the pasta and stir in the tomatoes, chilli, basil, extra virgin olive oil, salt and pepper. Serve sprinkled with cheese.

TIP The last person to be served is the luckiest, as they get the most sauce!

Two cheese sauce with pistachios and fettuccine

This is a rich and delicious sauce that can be made in minutes. Serve for special occasions.

200 g (7 oz) fettuccine

sea salt and freshly ground black pepper

150 ml (¼ pint) double cream

40 g (1½ oz) dolcelatte cheese

40 g (1½ oz) freshly grated Parmesan cheese

25 g (1 oz) shelled pistachio nuts

handful of fresh basil, torn, to garnish

SERVES 2

Illustrated in colour on page 57

1. Cook the pasta in a large saucepan of boiling salted water for 10 minutes until just tender.

2. Meanwhile, pour the cream into a saucepan and bring slowly to the boil. Reduce heat, crumble in the dolcelatte cheese and stir until melted and smooth. Add the Parmesan cheese. Cook over a low heat until thick and smooth.

3. Roughly chop the pistachio nuts. Add to the sauce and season with salt and pepper to taste.

4. Drain the pasta and stir in the sauce. Garnish with basil leaves and serve hot.

TIP The sauce can be made in advance then reheated just before serving. Store in the fridge for up to 2 days.

Roasted red pepper pesto with penne rigate

I love the dramatic colour of this sauce and it has a rich sweet flavour. It's fantastic with penne rigate as the ridges of this hollow pasta enable the sauce to cling to it.

Fills one 225 g (8 oz) jar.

4 medium red pepper

65 g (2½ oz) ground almonds

zest of 1 lemon, finely chopped

4 tablespoons extra virgin olive oil plus a little, to finish

1 garlic clove, skinned

2 teaspoons balsamic vinegar

50 g (2 oz) freshly grated Parmesan cheese

sea salt and freshly ground black pepper

penne rigate, to serve

fresh basil leaves, to garnish

SERVES 6

1. Preheat the oven to 200C (400F/Gas 6). Put the peppers on a baking sheet and roast in the oven for 25 minutes, turning them once during cooking. They should become charred and deflated. Remove and leave to cool on a wire rack. (This can be done the day before if wished).

2. The next stage of the pesto is very easy. When the peppers are cool, peel off the skin and remove the seeds. Try to save the precious pepper juice by holding them over a bowl.

3. Put the pepper flesh and all the other ingredients in the food processor and whizz until blended, smooth and thick. Taste and adjust seasoning if desired.

4. Put in a sterilised jar and top with olive oil to act as a preservative. Store in the fridge for up to 2 weeks.

5. Serve with freshly cooked penne rigate and garnish with basil leaves.

TIP The sauce is not only good with pasta but also makes an excellent salad dressing or can be served with freshly steamed vegetables.

Top: Roasted red pepper pesto with penne rigate.

Bottom: Two cheese sauce with pistachios and fettuccine (see page 55).

Roasted garlic, chilli and mushrooms with rigatoni

This sauce is easy to prepare and complements the pasta perfectly. Although there is one whole bulb of garlic per person, it is roasted until it is gently caramelised and is mild and sweet to eat. If you have never tried it before you are in for a wonderful – and very pleasant – surprise.

2 whole garlic bulbs
1 tablespoon olive oil plus a little, to drizzle
1 red chilli
150 g (5 oz) flat mushrooms
1 garlic clove, crushed
200 g (7 oz) rigatoni (ridged broad tube pasta)
150 ml (¼ pint) double cream
sea salt and freshly ground black pepper
freshly grated Parmesan cheese, to serve

SERVES 2

1. Preheat the oven to 200C (400F/Gas 6). Slice the top off the garlic bulbs and put in a roasting tin. Drizzle with a little oil and roast in the oven for 30 minutes, turning after 15 minutes. They will become golden and papery on the outside. Leave to cool slightly.

2. Finely chop the chilli discarding the seeds. Roughly chop the mushrooms. Heat the olive oil in a frying pan, add the mushrooms and fry for 8 minutes. Add the chilli and the crushed garlic clove and cook for a further 4 minutes.

3. Meanwhile, cook the pasta in a large saucepan of boiling salted water for 12 minutes until just tender.

4. Whilst the pasta is cooking, squeeze the roasted garlic cloves, like toothpaste from a tube, to extract the garlic pulp from each clove. Add the pulp to the mushroom mixture. Stir in the cream and add salt and pepper.

5. Drain the cooked pasta and pour over the sauce. Serve with the cheese.

TIP The garlic can be roasted the day before and kept, covered, in a cool place.

Fettuccine with chick peas

This is a classical Neapolitan dish. Chick peas are grown all over Italy but thrive in the south where it is sunny. If the chick peas are fresh the flavour of this dish is at its very best. The older the pulse, the longer it will take to cook and the flavour will not be as good. Although I think that dried pulses have more flavour and texture than canned, canned are definitely quick and easy and make a good substitute.

50 g (2 oz) dried chick peas

6 tomatoes

3 tablespoons olive oil

2 garlic cloves, crushed

handful of flat-leaved parsley, chopped

sea salt and freshly ground black pepper

200 g (7 oz) fettuccine or mezza zeta (pasta tubes)

6 fresh basil leaves, torn

freshly grated Parmesan cheese, to serve

SERVES 2

1. Soak the chick peas overnight, in a bowl of cold water..

2. The next day, drain the chick peas and put in a large saucepan. Cover with fresh water, bring to the boil and boil vigorously for 10 minutes. Lower the heat and simmer for 20 - 30 minutes, until tender. Drain well.

3. Put the tomatoes in a bowl, cover with boiling water for about 40 seconds then plunge into cold water. Using a sharp knife, peel off the skins then chop the flesh.

4. Heat 1½ tablespoons olive oil in a saucepan and gently fry the garlic. Add the tomatoes, parsley, chick peas, salt and pepper. Cover and set aside.

5. Cook the pasta in a large saucepan of boiling salted water for 10 minutes or until just tender. When cooked, drain and toss in the remaining olive oil then add to the chick pea mixture. Adjust seasonings to taste.

6. Serve sprinkled with the basil leaves and lashings of freshly grated Parmesan cheese.

TIP Dried pulses swell to double their weight once cooked. Always check the recipe to see whether it says cooked or dried as you could end up with mountains of chick peas as I have done before now!

Roasted fennel and tomato sauce with conchiglie

There is quite a different flavour from male and female fennels. The way to recognise a male from a female is quite simple. The male fennel is long and thin while the female is bulbous and has hips. The female fennel is quite fibrous and the flavour isn't quite as strong. In Italy, fennel is cut in thin strips and eaten as a digestive after meals. It is very alkaline and cleansing.

1 medium whole male fennel

8 tomatoes

3 tablespoons olive oil

1 garlic clove, crushed

grated rind of ½ a lemon

200 g (7 oz) conchiglie (pasta seashells)

sea salt and freshly ground black pepper

freshly grated Parmesan cheese, to serve

SERVES 2

1. Preheat the oven to 200C (400F/Gas 6). Trim the fennel and wash well. Cut into lengths then steam or cook in boiling water for 7 - 8 minutes until tender. Transfer to a roasting tin and drizzle over 1 tablespoon oil. Roast for 20 minutes until golden.

2. Meanwhile, put the tomatoes in a bowl, cover with boiling water for about 40 seconds, then plunge into cold water. Using a sharp knife, peel off the skins then chop the flesh, discarding the seeds.

3. Heat the remaining 2 tablespoons oil in a saucepan, add the garlic and fry gently. Add the tomatoes and lemon rind then cook gently for 25 minutes.

4. Chop the cooked fennel into small pieces and add to the sauce. Season with salt and pepper and heat gently.

5. Cook the pasta in boiling salted water for about 10 minutes until just tender.

6. When the pasta is cooked, drain and toss with the sauce. Serve hot with freshly grated Parmesan cheese.

Top: Roasted fennel and tomato sauce with conchiglie.

Bottom: Penne with broad beans and ricotta (see page 62).

Penne with broad beans and ricotta

Young broad beans are a real favourite of mine. The first of the season in Italy are removed from the pod, skinned and eaten raw as passatempi (to pass the time).

150 g (5 oz) shelled broad beans

200 g (7 oz) penne (short, hollow pasta)

1 tablespoon olive oil

1 garlic clove, crushed

25 g (1 oz) freshly grated pecorino cheese

50 g (2 oz) ricotta

about 2 tablespoons extra virgin olive oil

sea salt and freshly ground black pepper

fresh marjoram leaves, to garnish

SERVES 2

1. Steam the broad beans for 6 minutes until tender.

2. Meanwhile, cook the penne in a large saucepan of boiling salted water for 10 minutes until just tender.

3. Heat the olive oil in a saucepan and fry the garlic until coloured.

4. Drain the pasta and add to the pan with the broad beans, pecorino and ricotta, extra virgin olive oil, salt and pepper and toss well together. Serve garnished with marjoram leaves.

Illustrated in colour on page 61

Pasta and peas

This dish conjures up very happy memories for me at my Grandmother's home in Minori, Campania.

1 small onion

2 tablespoons olive oil

175 g (6 oz) shelled fresh peas

600 ml (1 pint) vegetable stock preferably home-made

150 g (5 oz) pappardelle (broad, ruffled edge pasta)

sea salt and freshly ground black pepper

handful of fresh basil leaves, torn

lashings of freshly grated Parmesan cheese

SERVES 2

1. Skin and finely chop the onion. Heat the oil in a medium saucepan, add the onion and fry until soft.

2. Add the peas and stock and cook for 10 minutes, until the peas are soft.

3. Add the pasta, broken into pieces, salt and pepper and cook for 12 minutes until pasta is tender (it will absorb some of the stock). Serve sprinkled with basil and Parmesan cheese.

TIP To eat this at its best, use fresh new season peas, when they are sweet and tender.

Cannelloni from Piacenza

These parcels of pasta, stuffed with spinach, ricotta, mascarpone and Parmesan cheese, are a very classical Italian dish and they taste fantastic! You make a rich batter and fry it in thin pancakes which you roll up with the filling.

PASTA

200 g (7 oz) plain white flour

sea salt

2 eggs, beaten

2 egg yolks

50 g (2 oz) butter, melted

about 300 ml (½ pint) milk

FILLING

900 g (2 lb) fresh tender spinach

handful of flat-leaved fresh parsley, finely chopped

150 g (5 oz) ricotta

100 g (4 oz) mascarpone cheese

65 g (2½ oz) freshly grated Parmesan cheese

1 egg, beaten

pinch of freshly grated nutmeg

sea salt and freshly ground black pepper

TO FINISH

50 g (2 oz) freshly grated Parmesan cheese

50 g (2 oz) butter

SERVES 4

1. To make the pasta, sift the flour and a pinch of salt into a bowl. Add the eggs, egg yolks and 1 tablespoon of melted butter, then gradually stir in the milk, adding enough to give a semi-liquid batter. Continue stirring for a further 10 minutes.

2. Heat 1 tablespoon of the remaining butter in a small, non-stick frying pan. Pour in just enough batter to cover the bottom, tilting the pan so that it spreads evenly. The pasta should be thin. Fry for 4 - 5 minutes on both sides, until golden. Remove from pan and turn on to a sheet of greaseproof paper. Repeat with the remaining mixture, adding more butter if necessary, to make 6 rounds.

3. Trim each pasta round to a rectangle. If wished, store, between sheets of greaseproof paper, in the fridge for up to 3 days.

4. To make the filling, wash the spinach and put in a saucepan with only the water still clinging to the leaves after washing. Cook for 5 minutes then drain well, squeezing out the excess water. Finely chop the spinach.

5. Put the spinach in a bowl, add all the other filling ingredients and beat together.

6. Preheat the oven to 200C (400F/Gas 6). Divide the filling between the pasta rectangles, placing it in the centre of each one. Fold the edges of each rectangle over the filling to form a parcel.

7. Arrange the cannelloni, in a single layer, in a buttered ovenproof dish. Sprinkle with Parmesan cheese. Melt butter and drizzle on top. Bake for 20 minutes until golden.

Brandelli with aubergine and courgette sauce

This is a firm family favourite – a delicious, fresh vegetable sauce simmered with red wine and rosemary. I love all the flavours and the richness from the wine adds a special something.

90 g (3½ oz) aubergine

sea salt and freshly ground black pepper

1 medium carrot

1 small courgette

1 small onion

2 tablespoons olive oil

1 garlic clove, crushed

1 teaspoon chopped fresh rosemary

100 ml (3½ fl oz) red wine

200 g (7 oz) brandelli (see Tip)

40 g (1½ oz) freshly grated pecorino cheese

SERVES 2

1. Peel the aubergine and chop the flesh into matchsticks. Put in a bowl and sprinkle with salt. Place a plate on top and weigh down. Leave for 20 minutes.

2. Meanwhile, cut the carrot and courgette into matchsticks. Skin and finely chop the onion. Rinse the aubergine matchsticks and pat dry.

3. Heat the olive oil in a saucepan, add the carrot, courgette and aubergine matchsticks and fry until golden. Add the onion and fry until coloured then add the garlic and rosemary. Lower the heat and add the wine, salt and pepper. Simmer, covered, for 5 minutes.

4. Meanwhile, cook the pasta in a large saucepan of boiling salted water for 12 minutes until just tender.

5. Drain the pasta and toss into the sauce. Serve sprinkled with pecorino cheese.

TIP Brandelli are crinkled square pasta shapes but if these are not available you could use pappardelle which are very broad noodles with ruffled edges or your favourite shape.

Brandelli with aubergine and courgette sauce.

Pizzoccheri

This is a very typical dish from Lombardy in Northern Italy, made with buckwheat pasta. The pasta is rolled into thin sheets and layered with a buttery potato and green vegetable mixture. In Lombardy it gets rather cold, so this is a warming dish.

PASTA

300 g (11 oz) buckwheat flour

150 g (5 oz) plain flour

3 eggs

7 tablespoons milk

salt

FILLING

200 g (7 oz) potatoes

225 g (8 oz) mixture of French beans and Brussels sprouts or cabbage

150 g (5 oz) unsalted butter

1 garlic clove, crushed

freshly grated nutmeg

handful of fresh sage leaves

sea salt and freshly ground black pepper

175 g (6 oz) fontina cheese, grated

100 g (4 oz) freshly grated Parmesan cheese

SERVES 6

1. To make the pasta, sift both the flours into a mound on to a work surface and make a hollow in the centre. Beat the eggs together and pour into the hollow with the milk, a little lukewarm water and a pinch of salt. Mix together to make a smooth dough, then leave to stand for 10 minutes.

2. Roll out the dough to a paper-thin sheet. Cut into strips, about 5 cm (2 in) long and 1 cm (½ in) wide.

3. To make the filling, peel and cube the potatoes then cook in boiling water until tender. Chop the cabbage, if using. Steam the vegetables until tender.

4. Heat the butter in a saucepan, add the garlic and fry gently until softened. Add the nutmeg, sage and vegetables and stir to coat vegetables in melted butter. Season well with salt and pepper.

5. Cook the pasta in a large saucepan of boiling salted water for 6 minutes until just tender. Drain well.

6. Put a layer of pasta and then vegetables in a warmed, large serving dish. Sprinkle with the fontina and Parmesan cheese. Repeat these layers and serve.

TIP As buckwheat pasta is hard to find, I've included a recipe to make it. Buckwheat flour can be bought from most health food shops.

Top: Pizzoccheri.

Bottom: Pasta Vesuvius (see page 68).

Pasta Vesuvius

Capers, olives, mint and cream give this dish rich Byzantine flavours from the south-western part of Italy. Mint features quite a bit in the food from the south and from Sicily. This is a real favourite of mine.

---

4 tomatoes

200 g (7 oz) fettuccine

sea salt and freshly ground black pepper

25 g (1 oz) stoned black or green olives

25 g (1 oz) capers

1 tablespoon olive oil

1 garlic clove, crushed

½ peperoncino, chopped (optional)

handful of flat-leaved parsley, finely chopped

handful of fresh mint, finely chopped

2 tablespoons mascarpone cheese

fresh mint and parsley sprigs, to garnish

SERVES 2

Illustrated in colour on page 67

1. Put the tomatoes in a bowl, cover with boiling water for about 40 seconds then plunge into cold water. Using a sharp knife, peel off the skins then chop the flesh, discarding the seeds.

2. Cook the pasta in a large saucepan of boiling salted water for 10 minutes until just tender.

3. Meanwhile, finely chop the olives and capers. Heat the oil in a saucepan and fry the garlic until softened. Add the olives, capers, tomatoes, peperoncino (if using), parsley and mint and fry gently for 5 minutes. Add the mascarpone cheese, salt and pepper.

4. Drain the pasta, add to the pan and toss together with Parmesan cheese. Garnish with sprigs of fresh mint and parsley and serve.

TIP For a special occasion, add a little double cream to the sauce at the end of step 3.

Ravioli with butter and sage

This ravioli is quite, quite special. I first enjoyed it in Umbria in a restaurant called 'Val Verde'. The ravioli is so light, it just melts in the mouth. I've subsequently eaten it all over Umbria and Emilia-Romagna.

PASTA

200 g (7 oz) strong white unbleached flour, preferably 'OO' grade

pinch of sea salt

2 large eggs

1 tablespoon olive oil

FILLING

100 g (4 oz) ricotta

50 g (2 oz) fontina cheese

50 g (2 oz) freshly grated Parmesan cheese

1 egg, beaten

pinch of freshly grated nutmeg

handful of fresh sage leaves, finely chopped

TO FINISH

50 g (2 oz) unsalted butter

a few fresh sage leaves, to garnish

freshly grated Parmesan cheese

SERVES 4

Illustrated in colour on page 70

1. Make the pasta dough as described on page 44.

2. Mix together all the filling ingredients and beat thoroughly.

3. Roll out the dough in a pasta machine. Alternatively, divide dough into manageable pieces and cover the dough you are not working with. Take 1 piece of dough and with the heel of your hand, press out the dough. Using a long, thin rolling pin and a little flour, roll out the dough to a paper thin sheet. Cut the pasta into 4 cm (1³/₄ in) squares. Place small spoonfuls of the filling on the squares 1 cm (½ in) from the edges, dampen the edges then fold the dough over the filling to make a triangle.

4. Cook the ravioli in a large saucepan of boiling salted water. Add a handful at a time and cook for about 5 minutes. When they rise to the top of the pan, count 30 seconds. With a slotted spoon, remove and place in a warmed serving dish.

5. Melt the butter and pour over the ravioli. Garnish with sage leaves and serve with a sprinkling of Parmesan cheese.

TIP These ravioli can be prepared in advance and kept in the fridge for up to 2 days.

Spinach, ricotta and tomato pasta rolls

In Umbria, the stylish presentation of this dish gives pasta a whole new slant. The filling is a classic, and very simple, blend of tender young spinach and ricotta cheese, flavoured with nutmeg. You roll the pasta into a large sheet, spread the filling over and roll it up Swiss-roll style.

PASTA

300 g (11 oz) strong white unbleached flour, preferably 'OO' grade

pinch of sea salt

2 large eggs

1 tablespoon olive oil

FILLING

4 tomatoes

350 g (12 oz) fresh spinach

175 g (6 oz) ricotta

freshly ground nutmeg

sea salt and freshly ground black pepper

TO FINISH

25 g (1 oz) butter

25 g (1 oz) freshly grated Parmesan cheese

SERVES 6

Top: Spinach, ricotta and tomato pasta rolls.

Bottom: Ravioli with butter and sage (see page 69)

1. Make the pasta as described on page 44.

2. Put the tomatoes in a bowl, cover with boiling water for about 40 seconds then plunge into cold water. Skin and chop the flesh.

3. Wash the spinach and put in a saucepan with only the water still clinging to the leaves after washing. Cook for 5 minutes then drain well, squeezing out the excess water.

4. Finely chop the spinach and put in a bowl. Add the tomatoes, ricotta, nutmeg, salt and pepper and mix together.

5. Roll out the dough to a rectangular sheet, about 3 mm (⅛ in) thick. Spread filling over dough, leaving a 3 cm (1¼ in) border. Roll up dough like a Swiss roll. Wrap in a piece of muslin and secure ends with string.

6. Place the roll in a long, narrow flame-proof casserole or roasting tin and cover with lightly salted cold water. Bring to the boil and simmer for 20 minutes. Remove from water and leave to cool for 5 minutes.

7. Remove the muslin and cut the roll into 2 cm (¾ in) thick slices. Place slightly overlapping, in a buttered, ovenproof dish.

8. Melt the butter and pour over the slices. Sprinkle with the Parmesan cheese and grill for 5 minutes. Serve immediately.

TIP The pasta roll can be made in advance and kept in the fridge for up to 2 days. Return to room temperature, slice and grill.

Bonbons filled with wild mushrooms and ricotta

These get their name because they look like sweets in wrappers with twisted ends. The mushroom and herb filling is light but flavourful. I make the bonbons in advance and cook them at the last minute. If I'm doing these for friends I make sure everyone is at the table before I put them on.

six 28 x 24 cm (11 x 9½ in) fresh plain pasta sheets

FILLING

200 g (7 oz) wild mushrooms

150 g (5 oz) flat mushrooms

½ an onion

150 g (5 oz) ricotta

2 tablespoons freshly grated Parmesan cheese

½ teaspoon finely chopped fresh sage

½ teaspoon finely chopped fresh oregano

½ teaspoon finely chopped fresh parsley

pinch of grated nutmeg

freshly ground black pepper

TO FINISH

1 egg, lightly beaten

a little single cream or melted butter, for coating

freshly grated Parmesan cheese

SERVES 6 AS A STARTER,
4 AS A MAIN DISH

1. Cut each pasta sheet into nine rectangles. Using a zigzag pastry wheel, trim shorter ends of each rectangle.

2. Finely chop the mushrooms and grate the onion. Mix all the filling ingredients together.

3. Place a teaspoon of filling in the centre of each pasta rectangle. Brush egg down one long side and fold pasta to form a tube. Press to seal then pinch and twist ends tightly, like bonbon wrappers. As each bonbon is made, set aside, uncovered, to rest.

4. Cook bonbons, a few at a time, in a large saucepan of boiling water for 4 - 5 minutes or until just tender. Remove with a slotted spoon and pile on to a warmed serving dish. Serve, tossed in cream or butter and sprinkled with Parmesan cheese.

TIP These Bonbons are best made with thinly rolled, home-made pasta. You will need to use 400 g (14 oz) of flour and 4 eggs; see the recipe on page 44.

Soup with pasta

This soup is warming, but not heavy, and is ideal for a light lunch on a cold day. Use a good stock for a fine flavour.

2 ripe tomatoes

450 ml (¾ pint) fresh vegetable stock

65 g (2½ oz) capelli d'angelo (fine long pasta)

sea salt and freshly ground black pepper

1 tablespoon extra virgin olive oil

25 g (1 oz) freshly grated Parmesan cheese

handful of flat-leaved parsley, finely chopped

SERVES 2

1. Put the tomatoes in a bowl, cover with boiling water for about 40 seconds then plunge into cold water. Using a sharp knife, peel off the skins then finely chop the flesh, discarding the seeds.

2. Bring the stock to the boil. Add the tomatoes and cook for 2 - 3 minutes.

3. Stir in the pasta and cook for 3 - 5 minutes until just tender. Season with salt and pepper to taste and stir in the olive oil. Serve sprinkled with Parmesan cheese and parsley.

Pasta with broccoli

Some of the best broccoli is grown in the south of Italy. Here I've combined it with pasta and home-made toasted breadcrumbs. To make these, spread day-old breadcrumbs on a baking sheet and bake at 190C (375F/ Gas 5), stirring frequently, until golden.

200 g (7 oz) ditali (short macaroni)

sea salt and freshly ground black pepper

375 g (13 oz) broccoli

50 g (2 oz) stoned green olives

2 tablespoons olive oil

1 garlic clove, finely chopped

50 g (2 oz) ground almonds

3 tablespoons freshly toasted breadcrumbs

a little extra virgin olive oil, to serve

freshly grated Parmesan cheese, to serve

SERVES 2

1. Cook the pasta in a large saucepan of boiling salted water for about 10 minutes, until just tender.

2. Meanwhile, cut broccoli into florets and steam for 6 minutes until tender.

3. Whilst the pasta and broccoli are cooking, finely chop the olives. Heat the oil and garlic in a frying pan. Add the olives and ground almonds and heat very gently. Add 1 tablespoon water.

4. Drain the cooked pasta. Toss in the broccoli, olive mixture and breadcrumbs and mix well together. Drizzle over some extra virgin olive oil and serve with Parmesan cheese.

Illustrated in colour on page 2

Tortellini with ricotta

Tortellini are a little fiddly to make so put some good music on in your kitchen, sit down and the job will become really pleasurable. The story goes that an innkeeper was attracted to a beautiful woman who came to stay at his inn. He peeped through the keyhole while she was undressing and saw her navel. He rushed downstairs to the kitchen and copied the shape in that night's fresh pasta. The shape he made is known as Tortellini.

PASTA

600 g (1 lb 6 oz) strong white unbleached flour, preferably 'OO' grade

pinch of sea salt

6 large eggs

1 tablespoon olive oil

semolina, for sprinkling

FILLING

150 g (5 oz) freshly grated Parmesan cheese, plus extra to serve

150 g (5 oz) ricotta

50 g (2 oz) truffle condiment

sea salt and freshly ground black pepper

knob of unsalted butter, to serve

TO FINISH

fresh basil leaves

SERVES 6

1. Make the pasta dough as described on page 44.

2. Mix together the Parmesan cheese, ricotta, truffle condiment, salt and pepper to taste.

3. Roll out the pasta dough in a pasta machine. Alternatively, divide dough into manageable pieces and cover the dough you are not working with. Take 1 piece of dough and with the heel of your hand, press out the dough. Using a long, thin rolling pin and a little flour, gently roll out the pasta to an even sheet that is almost paper-thin, sprinkling the surface with semolina. Cut the pasta into 10 cm (4 in) squares.

4. Place a teaspoonful of filling in the centre of each square. Moisten the edges with water then fold one corner over to make a triangle. Press the edges lightly together, bringing the corners of the triangle together to make a circular shape. Lay the tortellini on baking sheets, sprinkled with semolina, to dry for 1 hour.

5. Cook the tortellini in a large saucepan of boiling salted water for 4 - 5 minutes until just tender. Drain and serve with a little knob of butter, extra Parmesan cheese and garnish with basil leaves.

TIP Sprinkling the pasta with semolina, as you roll it out, helps the pasta to dry and therefore makes it easier to handle.

Tortellini with ricotta

Fried ravioli

Pasta is most often boiled or baked but deep frying is another excellent method of cooking. The pasta is crisp and delicious with a hot melted cheese middle flavoured with rocket and parsley. I hope you like my recipe.

PASTA

300 g (11 oz) strong white unbleached flour or plain white flour

sea salt

50 g (2 oz) unsalted butter

2 egg yolks

FILLING

100 g (4 oz) Gruyère cheese

75 g (3 oz) fresh rocket, finely chopped

40 g (1½ oz) freshly grated Parmesan cheese

1 egg, beaten

handful of flat-leaved fresh parsley, finely chopped

salt and freshly ground black pepper

TO FINISH

1 egg white

vegetable oil, for deep frying

SERVES 6

1. To make the pasta, sift the flour and a pinch of salt on to a work surface. Make a reservoir in the centre. Cut the butter into small dice and add with the egg yolks. Work to a smooth dough, adding a little lukewarm water if necessary.

2. To make the filling, grate the Gruyère cheese and put in a bowl with the rocket, Parmesan cheese, beaten egg, parsley and salt and pepper to taste. Stir well together.

3. Flatten the pasta dough with a rolling pin and roll out to a sheet about 5 mm (¼ in) thick. Cut into 12.5 cm (5 in) rounds. Divide the filling between the rounds, placing it in the centre of each one. Lightly whisk the egg white. Brush the edges of the round with a little egg white then fold the pasta over the filling to enclose it completely.

4. Deep fry the ravioli in hot oil, a few at a time, until golden brown. Drain on absorbent kitchen paper, while frying the remaining ravioli. Serve hot.

TIP The ravioli can be made in advance, stored in the fridge for up to 2 days, and cooked when needed.

Spaghetti with fresh tomato sauce

This recipe is for Maria who owns 'San Orsola', where I have taught, in Umbria. I have such happy memories of the summer, picking Maria's magnificent home-grown sweet, sun-ripened tomatoes. This simple dish is enjoyed all over Italy.

200 g (7 oz) spaghetti

sea salt and freshly ground black pepper

6 ripe tomatoes

2 garlic cloves, crushed

3 tablespoons olive oil

50 g (2 oz) freshly grated Parmesan cheese, plus extra to serve

handful of fresh basil leaves, torn

SERVES 2

1. Cook the spaghetti in a large saucepan of boiling salted water for about 10 minutes until just tender.

2. Chop the tomatoes and put in a bowl with the garlic, olive oil, Parmesan cheese, basil, salt and pepper and mix together.

3. Drain the pasta and toss with the sauce. Serve immediately with extra grated cheese if wished.

TIP Use the most ripe, red tomatoes available, to ensure maximum flavour.

Pasta with walnut sauce

This sauce should be made with fresh walnuts, still in the shell, if possible.

2 slices of bread

300 ml (½ pint) milk

300 g (11 oz) freshly shelled walnuts, if possible, or vacuum sealed walnuts

1 garlic clove, crushed

75 g (3 oz) freshly grated Parmesan cheese

6 tablespoons olive oil

handful of flat-leaved parsley

sea salt and freshly ground black pepper

400 g (14 oz) of your favourite pasta shapes

SERVES 4

1. Cut the crusts off the bread slices then leave the slices to soak in the milk for 10 minutes. Squeeze out the milk. Put the bread, walnuts, garlic, cheese, oil, parsley, salt and pepper in a food processor. Blend until smooth.

2. Cook the pasta in boiling salted water for about 10 minutes until just tender.

3. Gently reheat the sauce (do not boil). Drain the pasta and serve with the sauce.

TIP Store walnuts in the fridge or freezer to prevent them from becoming rancid.

Stuffed giant pasta shells

These filled pasta shells are fun to eat. They could be served with a white bechamel sauce but I think that they are excellent on their own.

350 g (12 oz) broccoli florets
50 g (2 oz) pine kernels
12 giant pasta shells
250 g (8 oz) dolcelatte cheese
1 garlic clove, crushed
small handful of finely snipped fresh chives
salt and freshly ground black pepper
a little extra virgin olive oil
freshly grated Parmesan cheese, for sprinkling

SERVES 2

1. Steam the broccoli florets for about 8 minutes until tender.

2. Toast the pine kernels on a sheet of foil under the grill, turning them frequently.

3. Cook the pasta shells in a large saucepan of boiling salted water for about 10 minutes until just tender.

4. Meanwhile, put the steamed broccoli, cheese, pine kernels, garlic, chives, salt and pepper in a bowl and mix together.

5. Drain the pasta and toss in a little olive oil to prevent them sticking together. Stuff with the filling whilst still warm.

6. Place the shells in a greased shallow ovenproof serving dish. Sprinkle over the Parmesan cheese and grill until bubbling. Serve immediately.

TIP Toasting the pine kernels makes them far tastier. Toast a large batch at one time and store in a jar in the fridge to keep them fresh.

Stuffed giant pasta shells

Squares of pasta with pesto

In Liguria, where this recipe originated, these are called Mandilli di Sea or silk handkerchiefs. This pesto is <u>the</u> recipe for Italy's classic basil and pine kernel sauce. Make it in the summer when basil is at its most tender, most fragrant and most prolific.

PASTA

200 g (7 oz) strong white unbleached flour, preferably 'OO' grade

pinch of sea salt

2 large eggs

1 tablespoon olive oil

PESTO

1 garlic clove, crushed

25 g (1 oz) pine kernels

sea salt

2 tablespoons freshly grated Parmesan cheese, plus extra to serve

50 g (2 oz) fresh basil leaves

75 ml (3 fl oz) fruity extra virgin olive oil

SERVES 2

1. Make the pasta dough as described on page 44.

2. Roll out the pasta dough in a pasta machine. Alternatively, divide dough into manageable pieces and cover the dough you are not working with. Take 1 piece of dough and with the heel of your hand, press out the dough. Using a long, thin rolling pin and a little flour, gently roll out the dough as thinly as you can. Leave it to dry on a clean tea-towel for 30 minutes. Cut the pasta into 15 cm (6 in) squares.

3. To make the pesto, using a pestle and mortar, pound the garlic, pine kernels and a pinch of salt together. Add the cheese and basil and continue to pound. Add the oil, a little at a time, and pound until you have a smooth paste.

4. Cook the pasta squares, 5 at a time, in boiling salted water for 7 minutes until just tender. Drain and toss the pasta with the sauce before serving hot with freshly grated Parmesan cheese.

TIP You may like to triple the quantity of pesto that you make and store in a jar for further use. Keep it in the fridge and always ensure that there is enough oil in the jar to cover the pesto, to prevent it from drying out.

Cannelloni with saffron sauce

After painstakingly making my own cannelloni by using a piping nozzle to stuff them, I have found this way of making cannelloni by far the easiest. I hope you will agree. The filling of cheeses, artichokes and rosemary is one of my favourites and the sauce – although very simple to make – tastes amazing. Do try it.

four 16 x 13 cm (6½ x 5 in) lasagne sheets

FILLING

1 small onion

50 g (2 oz) mozzarella cheese

4 canned artichoke hearts, drained and rinsed

2 tablespoons olive oil

100 g (4 oz) ricotta

50 g (2 oz) dolcelatte cheese

1 teaspoon finely chopped fresh rosemary

sea salt and freshly ground black pepper

SAUCE

15 g (½ oz) unsalted butter

½ garlic clove, crushed

1 g or a large pinch of pure saffron powder or strands

1 tablespoon white wine

125 g (4 oz) mascarpone cheese

sea salt and freshly ground black pepper

SERVES 2

1. Put the pasta in a large saucepan of boiling water. Return to the boil, boil for 1 - 2 minutes then drain and rinse under cold water.

2. To make the filling, chop the onion, mozzarella cheese and artichoke hearts. Heat the oil in a saucepan, add the onion and fry until soft. Add the chopped artichokes and cook for 5 minutes. Add the mozzarella, ricotta, dolcelatte cheese and rosemary. Season well with salt and pepper and mix well together.

3. To make the sauce, melt the butter in a saucepan, add the garlic and saffron and heat gently. Add the wine, mascarpone cheese, salt and pepper and simmer for 5 minutes.

4. Preheat the oven to 180C (350F/Gas 4). To assemble the dish, place some filling down the centre of each pasta sheet. Moisten the edges with water and roll the rectangle up its narrow edge to form a thick tube. Arrange cannelloni in a greased ovenproof dish. Pour sauce over and cover with foil.

5. Bake in the oven for 20 minutes. Serve immediately.

TIP Prepare the sauce the day before you are going to serve it, to allow the flavours to mature.

Country style rigatoni

This recipe captures the good, fresh flavours of the Italian countryside. It is one of my great mid-week stand-bys. The best sun-dried tomatoes are the ones without the seeds in because the seeds are bitter. Good sun-dried tomatoes should be slightly moist, sweet and tender.

1 tender young courgette

½ a red onion

½ a celery stick

4 stoned olives

2 sun-dried tomatoes

50 g (2 oz) Gorgonzola cheese

2 tablespoons olive oil

½ garlic clove, crushed

½ a glass of white wine

200 g (7 oz) rigatoni or any of your favourite pasta shapes

sea salt and freshly ground black pepper

handful of fresh basil leaves

freshly grated Parmesan cheese, to serve

SERVES 2

1. Chop the courgette into julienne strips. Finely chop the onion and celery. Roughly chop the olives. Chop the tomatoes. Cut the Gorgonzola cheese into cubes.

2. Steam the courgette strips for 2 minutes. In a medium saucepan, heat the oil and fry the onion for about 5 minutes until soft. Add the celery, garlic and wine and simmer for 6 minutes.

3. Meanwhile, cook the pasta in a large saucepan of boiling salted water for about 10 minutes until just tender.

4. Add the courgettes, olives, tomatoes, cubed cheese, basil, salt and pepper to the sauce and stir together.

5. Drain the pasta, add the sauce and toss together. Adjust seasonings to taste and serve immediately with Parmesan cheese.

TIP I always like to add a little extra olive oil at the end of cooking the pasta. I think it brings out the flavour of the sauce more.

Country style rigatoni

Polenta

POLENTA is a staple diet of Northern Italy. Basic polenta is made with polenta, which is maize flour, and salted water. In Italy, maize flour is known as farina gialla or granturco. It is available in a variety of forms – very coarse, medium or fine. The coarser the flour the more yellow in colour.

Whatever the type of flour used, polenta is always made in a special large copper pan called a 'paiolo'. The flour is gradually added to a pan of hot water and the mixture is stirred constantly throughout the cooking time, with a long wooden stick, to prevent lumps forming. The polenta is ready when it is like a thick porridge. It is then spread on to a wooden board and left to set.

Plain boiled polenta is rather bland, so it is often served with a strong flavoured sauce or with grated cheese. I like it best with ingredients, such as butter, herbs or garlic, added whilst it is cooking. Some of the best polenta dishes are those which have been cooked twice. The polenta is left to cool and when set it is fried or grilled and served with a sauce or topped with cheese and vegetables.

Cold polenta, cut into slices or chunks, is eaten as an alternative to bread in some parts of Northern Italy. It can also be eaten as a dessert, deep fried then tossed in sugar and lemon rind and served with mascarpone cheese.

Basic polenta

1 litre (1³/4 pints) vegetable stock (preferably home-made) or water

1 teaspoon sea salt

200 g (7 oz) coarse polenta

flavourings such as pepper, butter, chopped fresh herbs, crushed garlic, freshly grated Parmesan cheese

olive oil, for frying (optional)

SERVES 4

TIP I recommend using stock when making polenta as it adds more flavour to the dish.

1. In a large, heavy-based saucepan, bring the stock or water and the salt to the boil. Reduce to a simmer then gradually add the polenta, letting it run through your fingers in a thin stream, stirring constantly to prevent lumps forming.

2. Simmer for 30 - 40 minutes, until the mixture is thick and comes away from the sides of the pan, stirring frequently. Add flavouring of your choice and serve hot.

3. Alternatively, whilst the polenta mixture is still hot, spread it on to a dampened baking sheet or wooden board into a cake shape about 5 cm (2 in) thick. Leave for about 1 hour until set.

4. When cold, cut into 4 sections and then into 2.5 cm (1 in) thick slices.

5. Fry in olive oil for about 3 minutes on each side until crisp. Serve hot.

Polenta with butter and cheese

This is a simple way of serving polenta and makes a tasty lunch or supper dish.

600 ml (1 pint) vegetable stock or water

sea salt and freshly ground black pepper

125 g (4 oz) coarse polenta

75 g (3 oz) Gorgonzola cheese

50 g (2 oz) freshly grated Parmesan cheese

25 g (1 oz) butter (preferably unsalted)

SERVES 2

1. In a large saucepan, bring the stock or water and ½ teaspoon salt to the boil. Gradually add the polenta, stirring constantly. Simmer for 30 - 35 minutes, until the mixture comes away from the sides of the pan, stirring frequently.

2. Roughly chop the cheese and add to the polenta with the Parmesan cheese and butter. Stir together and serve hot.

Baked polenta with Gorgonzola and Taleggio cheese

Gorgonzola is my favourite blue cheese. Italians often eat blue cheese if they're run down as, they say, the natural penicillin in it gives them a boost.

1 litre (1¾ pints) vegetable stock or water

sea salt and freshly ground black pepper

200 g (7 oz) coarse polenta

50 g (2 oz) butter

125 g (4 oz) Gorgonzola cheese

125 g (4 oz) taleggio cheese

SERVES 2

TIP If the polenta spits during cooking, wrap a towel around your hand, as they do in Italy, to prevent it burning you.

1. In a large saucepan, bring the stock or water and 1 teaspoon salt to the boil. Gradually add the polenta, letting it run through your fingers in a fine stream, stirring constantly to prevent lumps forming. Simmer for 30 - 40 minutes, until the mixture is thick and comes away from the sides of the pan, stirring frequently. Stir in the butter and season with pepper.

2. Meanwhile, butter an ovenproof dish. Roughly chop the cheeses. Pour a layer of hot polenta into the dish. Add a layer of Gorgonzola, a layer of polenta, a layer of taleggio and finally a layer of polenta.

3. Preheat the oven to 220C (425F/Gas7). Bake the polenta for about 20 minutes until brown. Serve hot.

Pepper polenta

This polenta is speckled with piquant ingredients. I enjoyed it, in Venice, on a cold January day. It was most welcoming. In Italy, you would have polenta as a second course and then have vegetables afterwards. Italian food is very informal, and polenta seems to sum all that up for me.

---

2 red peppers

1.7 litres (3 pints) vegetable stock or water

sea salt and freshly ground black pepper

200 g (7 oz) polenta

25 g (1 oz) capers

65 g (2½ oz) stoned black olives

1 garlic clove, crushed

50 g (2 oz) freshly grated Parmesan cheese

50 g (2 oz) butter

handful of flat-leaved parsley, finely chopped

1 teaspoon finely chopped fresh oregano

2 tablespoons olive oil

SERVES 4

Illustrated in colour on page 84

1. Preheat the oven to 200C (400F/Gas 6). Put the peppers on a baking sheet and roast in the oven for 20 minutes, until deflated and slightly charred, turning once during cooking. Cover and leave to cool.

2. Meanwhile, in a large saucepan, bring the stock or water and 1 teaspoon salt to the boil. Gradually add the polenta, letting it run through your fingers in a thin stream, stirring constantly to prevent lumps forming. Simmer for 40 minutes, until the mixture comes away from the sides of the pan, stirring frequently.

3. When the peppers are cool enough to handle, peel off the skins. Chop the flesh, discarding the core and seeds. Chop the capers and olives.

4. When the polenta is cooked, stir in the peppers, capers, olives, garlic, Parmesan cheese, butter, parsley, oregano and pepper.

5. Whilst the polenta mixture is still hot, spread it on to a dampened baking sheet or wooden board to a 1 cm (½ in) thickness. Leave for about 1 hour until softly set.

6. When the polenta is cold, cut it into triangles. To serve, heat the oil in a frying pan and fry the triangles until crispy.

TIP I've chosen red peppers because I like the colour but there's no reason why you couldn't use green or yellow ones.

Polenta with fontina

This is a typical dish of Piemonte and Val d'Aosta. I love its subtle flavours and I hope you enjoy it too. Fontina cheese is a cows' cheese that melts beautifully to a soft, creamy texture.

1 litre (1³/4 pints) vegetable stock or water

sea salt and freshly ground black pepper

150 g (5 oz) coarse polenta

100 g (4 oz) fontina cheese

50 g (2 oz) freshly grated Parmesan cheese

65 g (2¹/2 oz) butter

SERVES 2 GENEROUSLY

1. In a large saucepan, bring the stock or water and 1 teaspoon salt to the boil. Gradually add the polenta, letting it run through your fingers in a fine stream, stirring constantly to prevent lumps forming.

2. Simmer the polenta for 30 - 40 minutes, until the mixture comes away from the sides of the pan, stirring frequently with a wooden spoon.

3. Meanwhile, grate the fontina cheese.

4. When the polenta is cooked, add the fontina cheese and season with pepper to taste. Pour the polenta into a shallow dish and sprinkle with the Parmesan cheese. Melt the butter and pour over the top of the polenta. Add a little more pepper and serve at once.

TIP If you are unable to buy fontina cheese, you could use Gruyère cheese instead.

Top: Polenta with fontina.

Bottom: Polenta skewers (see page 92).

Polenta skewers

I like these individual polenta skewers. They make great canapes or they can be served as starters.

---

1 litre (1³/4 pints) vegetable stock or water

sea salt and freshly ground black pepper

200 g (7 oz) coarse polenta

50 g (2 oz) butter

75 g (3 oz) freshly grated Parmesan cheese, plus extra for sprinkling

1 garlic clove, crushed

225 g (8 oz) cherry tomatoes

2 tablespoons olive oil

450 g (1 lb) flat mushrooms

2 sprigs of rosemary

100 g (4 oz) dolcelatte cheese

SERVES 8 AS A STARTER

Illustrated in colour on page 90

1. In a large saucepan, bring the stock or water and 1 teaspoon salt to the boil. Gradually add the polenta, stirring constantly. Simmer for 30 - 40 minutes until the mixture comes away from the sides of the pan, stirring frequently. Add the butter, Parmesan cheese, garlic and pepper.

2. Spread the hot mixture on to a dampened baking sheet to a 5 mm (¼ in) thickness. Leave for about 1 hour until set.

3. Meanwhile, preheat the oven to 200C (400F/Gas 6). Cut the tomatoes in half and place on a baking sheet. Drizzle with a little of the oil. Thickly slice the mushrooms and place on a baking sheet. Sprinkle with the remaining oil and place some rosemary on top. Bake the tomatoes and the mushrooms in the oven for 20 minutes.

4. Using a 2.5 cm (1 in) round cutter, cut the cold polenta into rounds. Cut the cheese into cubes.

5. Thread the halved tomatoes, mushrooms, polenta rounds and cheese on to cocktail or kebab sticks. Sprinkle with Parmesan cheese.

6. To serve, grill for about 7 minutes until golden.

TIP The Polenta skewers can be made the day before they are needed, stored in the fridge and grilled just before serving.

Baked polenta with tomatoes

There are so many variations of this dish but I think this is the best. Basically it is a bit like a lasagne with the polenta taking the place of the pasta. Let the dish rest when it comes out of the oven so that it will keep its layers when you serve it. My Cook's Tip is to season the dish well and, if you like, you can add roasted garlic purée (see page 58) and herbs to the polenta whilst it is cooking.

SAUCE

45 g (1½ oz) butter

1 small bay leaf

3 tablespoons plain flour

500 ml (16 fl oz) milk

freshly ground black pepper

pinch of freshly grated nutmeg

POLENTA

1 litre (1¾ pints) vegetable stock or water

sea salt

200 g (7 oz) coarse polenta

FILLING

400 g (14 oz) fresh tomatoes

300 g (11 oz) flat mushrooms

75 g (3 oz) butter

handful of fresh basil leaves, torn

75 g (3 oz) freshly grated Parmesan cheese

freshly ground black pepper

SERVES 4

1. To make the sauce, melt the butter in a saucepan. Add the bay leaf and stir in the flour. Cook over a medium heat for 1 minute. Remove from the heat and gradually stir in the milk until smooth. Season with pepper and nutmeg. Return to the heat and slowly bring to the boil, stirring constantly, until the sauce boils and thickens. Put greaseproof paper on top, to prevent a skin forming, and set aside.

2. To make the polenta, bring the stock or water and 1 teaspoon salt to the boil. Gradually add the polenta, letting it run through your fingers in a fine stream, stirring constantly to prevent lumps forming. Simmer for 40 minutes or until the mixture comes away from the sides of the pan, stirring frequently.

3. To make the filling, cover the tomatoes with boiling water for about 40 seconds then plunge into cold water. Skin then chop the flesh, discarding the seeds.

4. Thinly slice the mushrooms. In a frying pan, melt half the butter. Add mushrooms and cook until soft. Season with pepper.

5. Preheat the oven to 200C (400F/Gas 6). Remove polenta from the heat and stir in the remaining butter. Spread one-third of the polenta into a greased ovenproof dish. Top with one-third of the mushrooms, one-third of the tomatoes, the basil and one-third of the sauce. Repeat these layers twice then sprinkle with the Parmesan cheese.

6. Bake for 30 minutes until golden. Leave dish to rest before serving hot.

Rosemary and basil polenta

The marriage of these two herbs, with the subtle flavour of polenta is just great. This recipe is ideal served as a starter with the polenta served cold, cut into triangles with a fresh pesto to dip them in.

1 litre (1¾ pints) vegetable stock or water

sea salt and freshly ground black pepper

200 g (7 oz) coarse polenta

75 g (3 oz) freshly grated Parmesan cheese

50 g (2 oz) freshly grated pecorino cheese

50 g (2 oz) butter

2 teaspoons finely chopped fresh rosemary

handful of fresh basil, torn

Pesto, to serve (see Tip)

SERVES 8 AS A STARTER

1. In a large saucepan, bring the stock or water and 1 teaspoon salt to the boil. Gradually add the polenta, letting it run through your fingers in a thin stream, stirring constantly to prevent lumps forming. Simmer for 30 - 40 minutes, until the mixture comes away from the sides of the pan, stirring frequently.

2. When the polenta is cooked, stir in the Parmesan and pecorino cheese, butter, rosemary, basil and pepper.

3. Whilst the mixture is still hot, spread it on to a dampened baking sheet to a 1 cm (½ in) thickness. Leave for about 1 hour until set.

4. When set, cut into fingers and arrange attractively on a plate with the pesto in the centre. To eat, dip the fingers into the pesto.

TIP To make a quick PESTO, put 50 g (2 oz) basil leaves, 1 garlic clove, 25 g (1 oz) pine kernels, 2 tablespoons freshly grated Parmesan cheese, 75 ml (3 fl oz) extra virgin olive oil, salt and pepper in a food processor or blender and blend together to form a smooth sauce.

Rosemary and basil polenta

Polenta timballe

This dish is simple yet delicious. The polenta is well-flavoured with chives, parsley and mint, pressed into a spinach-lined loaf tin with a layer of fontina cheese in the middle. Served with a fresh tomato sauce, it is a cheerful dish with all the colours of the Italian flag.

250 g (8 oz) large spinach leaves

1 litre (1¾ pints) vegetable stock or water

sea salt and freshly ground black pepper

200 g (7 oz) coarse polenta

1 tablespoon snipped fresh chives

1 tablespoon finely chopped fresh parsley

1 tablespoon finely chopped fresh mint

25 g (1 oz) butter

2 garlic cloves, very finely chopped

1 egg white

150 g (5 oz) fontina cheese

Tomato sauce, to serve (see Tip)

SERVES 4

1. Grease a 23 x 12.5 cm (9 x 5 in) loaf tin. Wash the spinach and remove large stalks. Blanch in boiling water for 10 seconds then drain and dry. Use the leaves to line the loaf tin, leaving 2 cm (¾ in) to overhang the edge.

2. In a large saucepan, bring the stock or water and 1 teaspoon salt to the boil. Gradually add the polenta, letting it run through your fingers in a thin stream, stirring constantly to prevent lumps forming. Simmer for 30 - 40 minutes or until the mixture comes away from the sides of the pan, stirring frequently. Stir in the chives, parsley, mint, butter and garlic. Season with pepper to taste.

3. Preheat the oven to 180C (350F/Gas 4). Lightly beat the egg white with a fork and use to brush the spinach so that it will stick to the polenta. Spoon half the polenta mixture into the tin, pressing it down evenly. Grate the fontina cheese and sprinkle on top, leaving a 5 mm (¼ in) border. Cover with the remaining polenta mixture, pressing down firmly to smooth. Fold over the spinach to encase the loaf.

4. Bake in the oven for 30 minutes. Allow to rest for 5 minutes before slicing and serving with the Tomato sauce.

TIP To make a TOMATO SAUCE to serve with the Polenta Timballe, simply skin then chop 500 g (1 lb) fresh tomatoes, discarding the seeds. Heat 2 tablespoons olive oil in a saucepan, add 2 crushed garlic cloves and fry gently. Add the tomatoes, bring to the boil then cook gently for 25 minutes. Season with salt and pepper before serving.

Polenta with broccoli

This makes a stunning dish, vibrant in colour and texture. The broccoli is added to the polenta with the other flavourings. The polenta is left to cool in a pudding bowl and then cut into thick wedges.

1 litre (1¾ pints) vegetable stock or water

sea salt and freshly ground black pepper

200 g (7 oz) coarse polenta

175 g (6 oz) tiny broccoli florets

75 g (3 oz) freshly grated Parmesan cheese

75 g (3 oz) butter

½ a dried peperoncino, finely crushed

1 small garlic clove, crushed (optional)

3 tablespoons olive oil

Tomato sauce, to serve (see Tip page 96)

SERVES 4

1. In a large saucepan, bring the stock or water and 1 teaspoon salt to the boil. Gradually add the polenta, letting it run through your fingers in a thin steam, stirring constantly to prevent lumps forming.

2. Simmer the polenta for 30 - 40 minutes until the mixture comes away from the sides of the pan, stirring frequently.

3. Meanwhile, steam the broccoli florets for about 8 minutes until tender.

4. When the polenta is cooked, add the Parmesan cheese, butter, peperoncino, garlic if using, pepper and the broccoli.

5. Pour the mixture into a dampened 1.1 litre (2 pint) bowl and leave in a cool place for about 1 hour until set.

6. When cold, turn out the polenta and slice like a cake into 8 pieces. Brush oil on each slice of polenta and grill, preferably on a ridged grill pan, until slightly blackened and crispy. Serve immediately with the Tomato sauce.

TIP If liked, the Polenta can be sliced and served cold like a loaf of bread. Spread with butter and serve with cheese.

Polenta and mushrooms

This is another example of the versatility of polenta. Here it is used instead of bread as a base to mop up the juices from its red pepper, sage and mushroom topping. These are great served with a crisp green salad or as hot nibbles with drinks when you have friends round. I hope you like it.

1 red pepper

600 ml (1 pint) vegetable stock or water

sea salt and freshly ground black pepper

125 g (4 oz) coarse polenta

50 g (2 oz) freshly grated Parmesan cheese

50 g (2 oz) butter (preferably unsalted)

2 tablespoons olive oil

175 g (6 oz) flat mushrooms

100 g (4 oz) mozzarella cheese

handful of fresh sage leaves

SERVES 2

Polenta and mushrooms

1. Preheat the oven to 200C (400F/Gas 6). Put the pepper on a baking sheet and roast in the oven for 20 minutes, turning once.

2. Meanwhile, in a large saucepan, bring the stock or water and ½ teaspoon salt to the boil. Gradually add the polenta, stirring constantly. Simmer for 30 minutes, until the mixture comes away from the sides of the pan, stirring frequently.

3. When the pepper is cool enough to handle, peel off the skin. Cut the flesh into strips, discarding the core and seeds.

4. When the polenta is cooked, stir in the Parmesan cheese, butter and pepper.

5. Whilst the polenta mixture is still hot, spread it on to a dampened baking sheet or wooden board to a 1 cm (½ in) thickness. Leave for about 30 minutes until set.

6. Meanwhile, slice the mushrooms. Heat the oil in a frying pan, add the mushrooms and fry for 2 - 3 minutes. Grate the cheese.

7. When the polenta is cold, cut into 6.5 cm (2½ in) squares. Top the squares with some mozzarella cheese, red pepper strips, sage leaves and mushrooms.

8. To serve, cook under a grill until the cheese is bubbling.

TIP As a variation, steam sliced baby leeks, arrange on top of the polenta squares with dolcelatte cheese and grill.

Sun dried tomato polenta with rosemary

This is a real favourite of mine and they make excellent canapes. You get the softness of the polenta and the concentrated sweetness of the tomatoes speckled with basil and rosemary. I serve this with a rocket salad dressed with a good, fruity olive oil or with oven-roasted vegetables like peppers or fennel.

600 ml (1 pint) vegetable stock or water

sea salt and freshly ground black pepper

125 g (4 oz) coarse polenta

25 g (1 oz) sun dried tomatoes

50 g (2 oz) freshly grated Parmesan cheese

handful of fresh basil leaves, torn

1 teaspoon finely chopped fresh rosemary

50 g (2 oz) unsalted butter

SERVES 2

1. In a large saucepan, bring the stock or water and ½ teaspoon salt to the boil. Gradually add the polenta, letting it run through your fingers in a thin stream, stirring constantly to prevent lumps forming. Simmer for 30 - 35 minutes, until the mixture comes away from the sides of the pan, stirring frequently.

2. Meanwhile, chop the sun dried tomatoes. When the polenta is cooked, add the tomatoes with the Parmesan cheese, basil, rosemary, butter and pepper. Stir well together.

3. Whilst the polenta mixture is still hot, spread it on to a dampened baking sheet or wooden board to a 1 cm (½ in) thickness. Leave for about 45 minutes until set.

4. To serve, cut the cold, set polenta into squares and grill until golden. Serve hot.

TIP I also like to serve these polenta squares topped with cooked vegetables, such as aubergines or courgettes, and shavings of Parmesan cheese before grilling.

Spinach and onion polenta

This is a colourful, tasty way of eating polenta. I first enjoyed it in Verona when staying with friends and I thank them for this recipe. It makes a creamy, golden mash speckled with green and is very comforting food. I think of polenta as mountain food. It is to the Italians, what porridge is to the Scots. Polenta dishes are September to February food – warming and hearty to see you through the winter.

1.7 litres (3 pints) vegetable stock or water

sea salt and freshly ground black pepper

200 g (7 oz) coarse polenta

225 g (8 oz) fresh tender spinach

1 small onion

2 tablespoons olive oil

½ garlic clove, crushed

75 g (3 oz) freshly grated Parmesan cheese

50 g (2 oz) butter

olive oil, for frying (optional)

SERVES 4

1. In a large saucepan, bring the stock or water and 1 teaspoon salt to the boil. Gradually add the polenta, letting it run through your fingers in a thin stream, stirring constantly to prevent lumps forming. Simmer for 40 minutes, until the mixture comes away from the sides of the pan, stirring frequently.

2. Meanwhile, wash the spinach and put in a saucepan with only the water still clinging to the leaves after washing. Cook for 5 minutes then drain well, squeezing out the excess water. Chop the cooked spinach.

3. Skin and finely chop the onion. Heat the oil in a frying pan, add the onion and fry for 5 minutes until softened. Add the garlic and spinach and heat through for 4 minutes.

4. When the polenta is cooked, add the spinach mixture, Parmesan cheese, butter, salt and pepper to taste. Mix well together and serve immediately.

5. Alternatively, spread the polenta on to a dampened baking sheet or wooden board to a 1 cm (½ in) thickness. Leave for about 1 hour until set. When cold, cut into triangles and fry in olive oil until crispy.

TIP This polenta is good with a fresh Tomato sauce (see the Tip on page 96).

Fried polenta sandwiches

This is a special dish of Piemonte, a polenta sandwich with cheese in the middle which is deep fried in egg and breadcrumbs. In my first book, 'The 90s Vegetarian', I had a recipe for Fried Mozzarella Sandwiches which is a Neopolitan version. They are both delicious!

600 ml (1 pint) vegetable stock or water

sea salt and freshly ground black pepper

125 g (4 oz) coarse polenta

25 g (1 oz) freshly grated Parmesan cheese

25 g (1 oz) butter

100 g (4 oz) fontina cheese

1 large egg

flour, for dusting

175 g (6 oz) fresh breadcrumbs

olive oil, for frying

SERVES 2

1. In a large saucepan, bring the stock or water and ½ teaspoon salt to the boil. Gradually add the polenta, letting it run through your fingers in a thin stream, stirring constantly to prevent lumps forming. Simmer for 30 minutes, until the mixture comes away from the sides of the pan, stirring frequently.

2. When the polenta is cooked, add the Parmesan cheese, butter and pepper. Stir well together.

3. Whilst the polenta mixture is still hot, spread it on to a dampened baking sheet or wooden board to a 1 cm (½ in) thickness. Leave for about 45 minutes until set.

4. When the polenta is cold, cut into rounds using a 7.5 cm (3 in) cutter. Slice the fontina cheese the same size as the polenta rounds and sandwich a slice between 2 rounds of polenta. Press well together.

5. Beat the egg then dip the polenta sandwiches into flour, then the egg and finally the breadcrumbs.

6. Heat the oil in a frying pan and fry the sandwiches on both sides until golden brown. Serve immediately.

TIP Use a serrated knife to cut the polenta as this helps to hold the filling inside the sandwiches.

Fried polenta sandwiches

Polenta and beans

This is a speciality of Modena in Northern Italy. It is a very easy dish to prepare and ideal for a cold winter night. This is really hearty and soothing food and I eat it as an Italian version of beans on toast. Polenta makes a very good bread substitute.

---

75 g (3 oz) dried cannellini beans

1 litre (1³/4 pints) vegetable stock or water

sea salt and freshly ground black pepper

200 g (7 oz) coarse polenta

6 tomatoes

1 small onion

2 tablespoons olive oil

1 garlic clove, crushed

25 g (1 oz) butter

25 g (1 oz) freshly grated Parmesan cheese

SERVES 4

1. Soak the beans overnight, in a bowl of cold water.

2. The next day, drain the beans and put in a large saucepan. Cover with fresh water, bring to the boil and boil vigorously for 10 minutes. Lower the heat then simmer for 30 - 40 minutes until tender.

3. Meanwhile, in a large saucepan, bring the stock or water and 1 teaspoon salt to the boil. Gradually add the polenta, letting it run through your fingers in a fine stream, stirring constantly to prevent lumps forming. Simmer for 30 - 40 minutes until the mixture comes away from the sides of the pan, stirring frequently.

4. Put the tomatoes in a bowl. Cover with boiling water for about 40 seconds then plunge into cold water. Using a sharp knife, peel off the skins then chop the flesh, discarding the seeds.

5. Finely chop the onion. Heat the oil in a saucepan, add the garlic and onion and fry gently for 5 minutes until softened. When the beans are cooked, drain well and stir into the onion with the tomatoes.

6. When the polenta is cooked, stir in the butter, Parmesan cheese and bean mixture and serve hot.

TIP To save time you could use a 400 g (13 oz) can of beans instead of the dried beans.

Roman style polenta

This recipe is ideal served as a first course. The polenta is enriched with egg yolks which gives it a creamy texture and rounded flavour.

1 litre (1¾ pints) milk (or half milk and half water)

3 egg yolks

250 g (8 oz) coarse polenta

75 g (3 oz) butter

freshly ground nutmeg

sea salt and freshly ground black pepper

75 g (3 oz) freshly grated Parmesan cheese

SERVES 4 AS A STARTER

1. Pour the milk into a large, heavy based saucepan and bring just to below the boil. Lightly beat the egg yolks and mix in 2 - 3 tablespoons hot milk then set aside.

2. Gradually add the polenta to the hot milk, letting it run through your fingers in a thin steam, stirring constantly to prevent lumps forming. Add half the butter and season to taste with nutmeg, salt and pepper. Simmer for 30 - 40 minutes, until the mixture comes away from the sides of the pan, stirring frequently.

3. Remove from the heat and stir in 25 g (1 oz) Parmesan cheese, gradually stir in the egg mixture, then beat until smooth.

4. Whilst the polenta mixture is still hot, spread it on to a dampened baking sheet or wooden board to a 1 cm (½ in) thickness. Leave for about 1 hour until set.

5. When the polenta is cold, using a 4 cm (1½ in) cutter cut into rounds and arrange, slightly overlapping, in a greased, shallow ovenproof dish.

6. Preheat the oven to 200C (400F/Gas 6). Melt the remaining butter and drizzle over the polenta. Sprinkle with the remaining Parmesan cheese and bake in the oven for 15 minutes or until golden. Serve hot.

TIP Prepare the polenta the day before it is needed then cut and bake it just before serving.

Wild mushroom and wine polenta

Wild mushrooms have grown in popularity in this country and mushroom hunts too, are becoming more and more popular. If, however, you are picking them yourself, it is important to always pick them with an expert.

sea salt and freshly ground black pepper

200 g (7 oz) coarse polenta

50 g (2 oz) butter

50 g (2 oz) freshly grated Parmesan cheese

700 g (1½ lb) wild or cultivated flat mushrooms

4 tablespoons olive oil

1 small garlic clove

1 tablespoon chopped fresh thyme

150 ml (¼ pint) white wine

2 tablespoons chopped flat-leaved parsley

SERVES 4

1. In a large saucepan, bring 1.7 litres (3 pints) water and 1 teaspoon salt to the boil. Gradually add the polenta, letting it run through your fingers in a thin stream, stirring constantly to prevent lumps forming. Simmer for 40 minutes, until the mixture comes away from the sides of the pan, stirring frequently.

2. When the polenta is cooked, stir in the butter and cheese and season with pepper.

3. Whilst the polenta is still hot, spread it on to a dampened baking sheet or wooden board into a mound. Leave for about 1 hour until softly set.

4. Cut any large mushrooms into quarters. Heat the oil and garlic in a saucepan. When the aroma rises, add the mushrooms and thyme and cook over a high heat for 1 minute. Season with salt and pepper. Add the wine and boil vigorously until it almost evaporates. Stir in the parsley.

5. Serve the mushrooms with slices of the polenta.

TIP For a special occasion, add 2 tablespoons double cream to the cooked mushrooms.

Wild mushroom and wine polenta

Polenta with fennel

I have a great fondness for fennel. This dish has a delicate flavour and only needs a crisp salad to accompany it. The polenta is slightly textured as you only cook the fennel lightly.

1.7 litres (3 pints) vegetable stock or water

sea salt and freshly ground black pepper

200 g (7 oz) coarse polenta

1 male fennel head

50 g (2 oz) Gruyère cheese

50 g (2 oz) freshly grated Parmesan cheese

50 g (2 oz) butter

2 tablespoons double cream

½ teaspoon fennel seeds, crushed

SERVES 4

1. In a large saucepan, bring the stock or water and 1 teaspoon salt to the boil. Gradually add the polenta, letting it run through your fingers in a thin stream, stirring constantly to prevent lumps forming. Simmer for 40 minutes, until the mixture comes away from the sides of the pan, stirring frequently.

2. Meanwhile, trim the fennel and wash well. Chop into small pieces then steam for 4 minutes until tender. Grate the Gruyère cheese.

3. When the polenta is cooked, stir in the fennel, Gruyère and Parmesan cheese, butter, cream, fennel seeds and pepper. Serve immediately.

4. Alternatively, whilst the polenta is still hot, turn on to a dampened baking sheet or wooden board and spread into a mound. Leave for about 1 hour until softly set. To serve, cut the polenta into slices and grill or fry until crisp. Serve hot.

TIP Always buy the long, tall male fennel. This is not as stringy as the female fennel, which is bulbous.

Polenta with milk

This is a nourishing way of eating polenta and, in Italy, is often given to children.

---
sea salt

125 g (4 oz) coarse polenta

grated rind of 1 lemon

275 ml (9 fl oz) milk or 100g (4 oz) ricotta

sugar, for sprinkling (optional)

SERVES 2

1. In a large saucepan, bring 600 ml (1 pint) water and a pinch of salt to the boil. Gradually add the polenta, stirring constantly. Simmer for 30 minutes, until the mixture comes away from the sides of the pan, stirring frequently.

2. When the polenta is cooked, add the lemon rind. Turn into bowls and serve with milk or ricotta and sugar if desired.

Polenta with dark chocolate and toasted hazelnuts

This is for a special treat and is extra good served with mascarpone cheese.

---
200 g (7 oz) coarse polenta

175 g (6 oz) plain chocolate

75 g (3 oz) hazelnuts, toasted

icing sugar, to dust

SERVES 4

1. In a large saucepan, bring 1 litre (1¾ pints) water to the boil. Reduce to a simmer then gradually add the polenta, letting it run through your fingers in a fine stream, stirring constantly to prevent lumps forming. Simmer for 30 - 40 minutes, until the mixture comes away from the sides of the pan, stirring frequently.

2. Meanwhile, butter a shallow dish. Chop the chocolate into small pieces and roughly chop the hazelnuts. Add the chocolate and hazelnuts to the cooked polenta and stir until chocolate has dissolved. Pour into the dish and leave for 30 - 40 minutes until set.

3. Serve, warm or cold, sprinkled with icing sugar.

Candied fruit polenta

The candied fruit in this recipe is soaked in brandy. This makes it delicious on its own but for sheer indulgence serve topped with a spoonful of mascarpone cheese. It is traditionally a festive polenta and when I made this at Christmas time for my students in Italy they were very enthusiastic about it.

100 g (4 oz) chopped peel (see Tip)

50 g (2 oz) sultanas

3 wine glasses of brandy

200 g (7 oz) coarse polenta

50 g (2 oz) caster sugar

2 eggs

25 g (1 oz) toasted pine kernels

pinch of ground mixed spice

pinch of ground cinnamon

grated rind of 1 lemon

olive oil, to fry (optional)

icing sugar, to serve (optional)

SERVES 2

1. Soak the candied peel and sultanas overnight, in 2 wine glasses of brandy.

2. In a large saucepan, bring 1.7 litres (3 pints) water to the boil. Gradually add the polenta, letting it run through your fingers in a thin stream, stirring constantly to prevent lumps forming. Simmer for 40 minutes, until the mixture comes away from the sides of the pan, stirring frequently.

3. When the polenta is cooked, stir in the soaked fruit, remaining brandy, sugar, eggs, pine kernels, mixed spice, cinnamon and lemon rind and mix well together. Serve immediately.

4. Alternatively, spread on to a dampened baking sheet or wooden board to a 2.5 cm (1 in) thickness. Leave for about 1 hour until softly set. When cold, cut the polenta into fingers and fry in oil until crisp. Serve warm, sprinkled with icing sugar.

TIP Try to buy whole pieces of candied peel and chop the peel yourself as it has a much better flavour than the tubs of chopped peel you can buy.

Candied fruit polenta

Index

Artichoke and Gorgonzola Pizza 18
Asparagus Calzone 20
aubergines 17
 Aubergine and Ricotta Pizza 17
 Brandelli with Aubergine and Courgette Sauce 65
 Mint Pesto and Aubergine Pizza 23

Baked Polenta with Tomatoes 93
basil
 Ricotta Focaccia with Basil 33
 Rosemary and Basil Polenta 94
Bonbons with Mushrooms and Ricotta 72
Brandelli with Aubergine and Courgette Sauce 65
broccoli
 Pasta with Broccoli 73
 Polenta with Broccoli 97
buckwheat pasta 66

Candied Fruit Polenta 110
cannelloni
 from Piacenza 63
 with Saffron Sauce 81
Char-grilled Vegetable Pizza 16
Chick Peas with Fettuccine 59
Conchiglie with Fennel and Tomato Sauce 60
courgettes
 Pizza with Courgette Flowers 25

ditali 73
dough
 for focaccia 31
 for pasta 44-47
 for pizza 12-15

fennel
 Fennel and Tomato Sauce with Conchiglie 60
 Polenta with Fennel 108
fettuccine 49
 with Chick Peas 59
 Pasta Vesuvius 68
 Two Cheese Sauce with Pistachios 55
Flat Bread with Grapes 41

Flat Bread with Olives 37
flour
 for pasta 43, 66
 for pizza 11
 for polenta 85
Focaccia 31
 Flat Bread with Olives 37
 Oil and Sage 36
 Ricotta and Basil 33
 Spinach, Olive and Onion 32
 Tomato, Onion and Rocket 34
folded pizza
 Asparagus Calzone 20
 Folded Onion Pizza 29
Four Cheese Pizza 24
Fried Polenta Sandwiches 102
Fried Ravioli 76
Fusilli with Gorgonzola and Pine Kernels 50

garlic
 Garlic, Chilli and Mushroom Rigatoni 58
 Pasta with Garlic & Oil 54
Goats' Cheese Pizza 28
Gorgonzola and Artichoke Pizza 18
Gorgonzola and Pine Kernels with Rigatoni 50
Gorgonzola and Taleggio Baked Polenta 88

macaroni 49
 Pasta with Broccoli 73
maize flour 85
Mint Pesto and Aubergine Pizza 23
mushrooms
 Bonbons with Mushrooms and Ricotta 72
 Garlic, Chilli and Mushrooms with Rigatoni 58
 Mushroom and Wine Polenta 107
 Pizza Norcina 26
 Polenta and Mushrooms 99

olives
 Flat Bread with Olives 37
 Spinach, Olive and Onion Focaccia 32
onions
 Onion Pizza 29

Shallot Pizza 21
orecchiette 49
 Pasta with Turnip Tops 51

pappardelle 49
 with Aubergine and Courgette Sauce 65
 Pasta and Peas 62
 with Truffles and Porcini 53
pasta 43-82
 dough preparation 44-47
 pasta shapes 48-49
 with Broccoli 73
 with Garlic and Oil 54
 and Peas 62
 with Pesto 80
 with Turnip Tops 51
 Pasta Vesuvius 68
 with Walnut Sauce 77
penne 49
 with Broad Beans and Ricotta 62
 with Roasted Red Pepper Pesto 56
Pepper Polenta 89
pesto
 quick pesto 94
 Mint Pesto and Aubergine Pizza 23
 Red Pepper Pesto with Penne 56
 Squares of Pasta with Pesto 80
Pitta (yeasted pie) 39
pizza 11-41
 dough preparation 12-15
 Pizza Norcina 26
Pizzoccheri 66
polenta 85-110
 basic polenta 86-87
 and Beans 104
 with Broccoli 97
 with Butter and Cheese 88
 with Chocolate and Hazelnuts 109
 with Fennel 108
 with Fontina 91
 with Milk 109
 and Mushrooms 99
 Polenta Skewers 92
 Polenta Timballe 96
 Roman Style 105
 Rosemary and Basil 94
 Spinach and Onion 101
 Tomato with Rosemary 100

Potato Pizza 40
ravioli 48
 with Butter and Sage 69
 Fried Ravioli 76
Red Pepper Pesto with Penne 56
Ricotta Focaccia with Basil 33
rigatoni 49
 Country Style 82
 with Garlic, Chilli and Mushrooms 58
 with Gorgonzola and Pine Kernels 50
Roasted Garlic, Chilli and Mushroom Rigatoni 58

Shallot Pizza 21
Soup with Pasta 73
spaghetti 48, 49
 with Cheese and Pepper 53
 with Fresh Tomato Sauce 77
 Pasta with Garlic and Oil 54
 with Tiny Tomatoes 54
spinach
 Spinach, Olive and Onion Focaccia 32
 Spinach and Onion Polenta 101
 Spinach, Ricotta and Tomato Pasta Rolls 71
Stuffed Giant Pasta Shells 79
Sun dried Tomato Polenta with Rosemary 100

tagliatelle 48, 49
 pasta preparation 46
Tomato, Onion and Rocket Focaccia 34
Tomato Pizza 24
Tomato and Rosemary Polenta 100
tomato sauce 96
Tortellini with Ricotta 74
truffles 26
 Pappardelle with Truffles and Porcini 53
Two Cheese Sauce with Pistachios & Fettuccine 55

Vegetable Pizza 16

Walnut Sauce 77
Wild Mushroom and Wine Polenta 107